Today's Italian Touch
from
PROGRESSO®

Introduction

Progresso invites you to join us in appreciation of good food and quality ingredients. We hope that you truly will enjoy using Progresso products in home-style dishes that will help to bring Italian-style family tradition into your home.

Nearly a century of Italian-American family heritage forms a strong foundation for the fine soups, sauces, bread crumbs, appetizers and olive oils that make up the Progresso family. Their rich, authentic tastes and textures are based on traditional Old World recipes that celebrate a love of life and reflect a deeply rooted passion for food.

Progresso began in New Orleans at the turn of the century when a young Italian immigrant began importing olive oil, tomato products and other essentials for the Italian-American community. Throughout the years, the Progresso family of products has continued to expand. Progresso now features more than 40 varieties of soup, a wide range of tomato, spaghetti and pasta sauces, seafood sauces, bread crumbs, olive oils, wine vinegars, spices and specialties, from antipasto to marinated mushrooms and asparagus.

Today, Progresso's unwavering commitment to quality and flavor remains the company's top priority. From selecting just the right pasta for a soup to simmering one of our sauces, everything we do is to ensure the taste of homemade goodness.

This commitment, combined with the following carefully developed and tested recipes, makes it easy for you to create rich and robust or delicate and light dishes that will bring the Old World celebration of food into your home.

Antipasti

Chicken Fingers Italiano

Kids of all ages will love these zesty chicken sticks dipped into their favorite sauce.

1 pound boneless, skinless chicken breast halves, pounded to ¼-inch thickness
1 egg, lightly beaten
¾ cup PROGRESSO Italian Style Bread Crumbs
¼ cup PROGRESSO Olive Oil

1. Cut chicken into strips.

2. Dip chicken into egg; coat with bread crumbs.

3. In large skillet, heat oil over medium heat. Cook chicken 6 minutes or until browned on both sides and no longer pink in center. Serve with your choice of dipping sauces.   Makes 8 appetizer servings

Estimated preparation time: 20 minutes
Cooking time: 6 minutes

Per serving: 177 calories, 15g protein, 9g fat (46% of calories), 8g carbohydrate, 59mg cholesterol, 225mg sodium, ‹1g dietary fiber

Suggested Dipping Sauces: PROGRESSO Marinara Sauce, mayonnaise/mustard, horseradish, sweet and sour sauce, honey

Chicken Fingers Italiano

Spicy Clam Dip

A lively flavored dip you can make ahead.

1 can (6½ ounces) PROGRESSO Minced Clams, drained
1 cup sour cream
2 tablespoons PROGRESSO Tomato Paste
2 tablespoons chopped onion
2 tablespoons chopped celery
2 teaspoons lemon juice
¼ teaspoon cayenne pepper
¼ teaspoon dill weed
¼ teaspoon salt

1. In small bowl, combine all ingredients; mix well.

2. Chill 2 hours. Serve with crackers or fresh vegetable dippers.

Makes 1¼ cups

Estimated preparation time: 15 minutes
Chilling/cooling time: 2 hours

Per 2 tablespoon serving: 75 calories, 5g protein, 5g fat (62% of calories),
3g carbohydrate, 20mg cholesterol, 136mg sodium, ‹1g dietary fiber

Crostini

Crisp and fragrant, this flavorful appetizer helps bring home
the atmosphere of an Italian trattoria.

½ cup PROGRESSO Olive Oil
2 tablespoons minced garlic
1 loaf (1 pound) Italian bread, cut into 3×3-inch pieces, ¼ inch thick
2 cups of your favorite topping, chopped*
2 cups (8 ounces) shredded cheese**
2 teaspoons dried oregano leaves

1. In small skillet, heat olive oil. Add garlic; cook 1 minute.

2. Place bread on large baking sheet. Brush one side of each slice
   generously with olive oil mixture. Broil until lightly toasted.

3. Turn bread slices over; brush untoasted side with remaining olive oil
   mixture.

4. Spoon topping onto each slice; sprinkle with cheese and oregano.

5. Broil until cheese is melted and edges of bread are golden brown.

Makes about 3 dozen

Estimated preparation time: 10 minutes
Baking time: 5 minutes

Per 2 slice serving (each with 1½ tablespoons marinated mushrooms and 1 tablespoon mozzarella cheese): 259 calories, 7g protein, 19g fat (64% of calories), 17g carbohydrate, 9mg cholesterol, 381mg sodium, 1g dietary fiber

* **Topping Suggestions:** Any one or combination of PROGRESSO Marinated Mushrooms, PROGRESSO Pepper Salad, PROGRESSO Tuscan Peppers (pepperoncini), PROGRESSO Roasted Peppers (red), PROGRESSO Imported Capers, anchovies, pepperoni

** **Cheese Suggestions:** Any one or combination of mozzarella, provolone, fontinella, Italian sharp

Mozzarella-in-the-Middle Rice Balls

A unique flavor and texture combination—crunchy fried rice balls filled with melted mozzarella.

  2 cups cold cooked rice
  ½ cup PROGRESSO Grated Parmesan Cheese
  ¼ cup finely chopped PROGRESSO Roasted Peppers (red)
  1 egg, lightly beaten
  ½ teaspoon salt
  ¼ teaspoon ground black pepper
  8 (½-inch) cubes mozzarella cheese
  ½ cup PROGRESSO Italian Style Bread Crumbs
    PROGRESSO Olive Oil for deep frying

1. In medium bowl, combine rice, Parmesan cheese, roasted peppers, egg, salt and pepper.

2. Shape rice balls using ⅓ cup rice mixture for each ball. Gently insert cheese cube into center of each ball; reshape rice mixture around cheese cube to cover completely.

3. Coat balls with bread crumbs.

4. In heavy 3-quart saucepan, heat 2 inches olive oil (approximately 6 cups) to 365°F. Deep fry balls, in small batches, 5 minutes or until golden brown on all sides. Remove with slotted spoon; drain on paper towels. Serve immediately with heated PROGRESSO Marinara Sauce, if desired.

Makes 4 appetizer servings

Estimated preparation time: 10 minutes
Cooking time: 10 minutes

Per 2 rice ball serving: 534 calories, 14g protein, 37g fat (59% of calories), 43g carbohydrate, 69mg cholesterol, 780mg sodium, 1g dietary fiber

Fried Pasta with Marinara Sauce

These crunchy, fried pasta dippers will be the hit at any party.

PROGRESSO Olive Oil for deep frying
½ cup PROGRESSO Grated Parmesan Cheese
¼ cup PROGRESSO Italian Style Bread Crumbs
1 package (7 ounces) spiral-shaped pasta, cooked according to package directions
1 cup PROGRESSO Marinara Sauce, heated

1. In heavy 2-quart saucepan, heat 1½ inches olive oil (approximately 3 cups) to 350°F.

2. In small bowl, combine Parmesan cheese and bread crumbs; set aside.

3. Deep fry pasta, in small batches, 4 minutes or until crunchy and lightly browned. Remove with slotted spoon; drain on paper towels. Add to cheese mixture; toss lightly to coat. Serve immediately with marinara sauce.   Makes 4 appetizer servings

Estimated preparation time: 15 minutes
Cooking time: 16 minutes

Per serving: 436 calories, 10g protein, 35g fat (71% of calories), 23g carbohydrate, 27mg cholesterol, 616mg sodium, 1g dietary fiber

Toasted Ravioli

Serve crisp ravioli with heated marinara sauce as an appetizer or main dish.

Vegetable oil for deep frying
24 meat- or cheese-filled ravioli, thawed, if frozen
2 eggs, lightly beaten
¾ cup PROGRESSO Italian Style Bread Crumbs

1. In heavy 1½-quart saucepan, heat 1 inch vegetable oil (approximately 2 cups) to 350°F.

2. Dip ravioli into eggs; coat with bread crumbs.

3. Deep fry ravioli, in small batches, 1 minute or until golden brown. Remove with slotted spoon; drain on paper towels.
                            Makes 8 appetizer servings

Estimated preparation time: 10 minutes
Cooking time: 5 minutes

Per serving (meat filled): 195 calories, 6g protein, 8g fat (42% of calories), 21g carbohydrate, 75mg cholesterol, 329mg sodium, ‹1g dietary fiber

Fried Pasta with Marinara Sauce

Cocktail Meatballs Italian-Style

A hearty appetizer with a wonderful Italian flavor. You can make and brown the meatballs ahead, then simmer them in the sauce just before the party.

1 pound ground beef
¾ cup PROGRESSO Italian Style Bread Crumbs, divided usage
½ cup chopped onion
¼ cup PROGRESSO Grated Parmesan Cheese
½ cup water
1 egg, lightly beaten
1 clove garlic, minced
½ teaspoon salt
⅛ teaspoon ground black pepper
¼ cup PROGRESSO Olive Oil
1 can (15 ounces) PROGRESSO Tomato Sauce
⅓ cup packed brown sugar
½ cup PROGRESSO Red Wine Vinegar

1. In large bowl, combine ground beef, ¼ cup bread crumbs, onion, Parmesan cheese, water, egg, garlic, salt and pepper.

2. Shape meatballs using 1 level tablespoon meat mixture for each meatball; coat with remaining ½ cup bread crumbs.

3. In large skillet, heat olive oil. Add meatballs. Cook 5 to 7 minutes or to desired doneness, turning occasionally to brown on all sides. Drain.

4. In small bowl, combine tomato sauce, brown sugar and vinegar; pour over meatballs. Cover; simmer 20 minutes, stirring occasionally.

Makes about 3 dozen

Estimated preparation time: 45 minutes
Cooking time: 30 minutes

Per 2 meatball serving: 144 calories, 8g protein, 9g fat (53% of calories), 9g carbohydrate, 36mg cholesterol, 298mg sodium, ‹1g dietary fiber

Microwave Directions: Omit olive oil. Prepare meatballs as directed above in Steps 1 and 2. In shallow 2-quart microwave-safe casserole, place meatballs in single layer. Microwave on HIGH (100% power) 7 to 8 minutes or to desired doneness, rotating dish after 4 minutes; drain. In small bowl, combine tomato sauce, brown sugar and vinegar; pour over meatballs. Cover. Microwave on MEDIUM (50% power) 9 minutes or until thoroughly heated, stirring every 4 minutes.

Cocktail Meatballs Italian-Style

Fried Cheese Nuggets

Here's an easy way to dazzle your family and friends: rich melted cheese, encased in crisp, golden bread crumbs and complemented with a zesty tomato sauce.

Vegetable oil for deep frying
8 ounces provolone cheese
8 ounces mozzarella cheese
3 egg whites, lightly beaten
2 tablespoons water
½ cup all-purpose flour
1½ cups PROGRESSO Italian Style Bread Crumbs
1 jar (14 ounces) PROGRESSO Marinara Sauce, heated

1. In heavy 2-quart saucepan, heat 2 inches vegetable oil (approximately 4 cups) to 350°F.

2. Cut cheese into ¼×½×1-inch pieces.

3. In small bowl, combine egg whites and water.

4. Dip cheese into flour, then into egg mixture. Coat with bread crumbs.

5. Deep fry cheese, in small batches, 15 to 20 seconds or until golden brown. Remove with slotted spoon; drain on paper towels. (Remove crumbs from oil with slotted spoon as necessary.) Serve immediately with marinara sauce. Makes 10 appetizer servings

Estimated preparation time: 10 minutes
Cooking time: 10 minutes

Per serving: 312 calories, 17g protein, 18g fat (51% of calories), 22g carbohydrate, 29mg cholesterol, 772mg sodium, 1g dietary fiber

Spinach Balls Parmesan

Shape the spinach balls ahead, then fry them when ready to serve. A great party finger food.

2 packages (10 ounces each) frozen chopped spinach, cooked according to package directions and well drained
1⅓ cups PROGRESSO Italian Style Bread Crumbs
⅓ cup PROGRESSO Grated Parmesan Cheese
¼ cup finely chopped celery
¼ cup finely chopped onion
½ teaspoon hot pepper sauce
¼ teaspoon nutmeg
2 eggs, lightly beaten
PROGRESSO Olive Oil for deep frying

1. In large bowl, combine spinach, bread crumbs, Parmesan cheese, celery, onion, hot pepper sauce, nutmeg and eggs; mix well.

2. Shape spinach mixture into balls using 1 level tablespoon mixture for each ball.

3. In heavy 2-quart saucepan, heat 1¼ inches olive oil (approximately 3 cups) to 350°F. Deep fry balls, in small batches, 1 minute or until golden brown. Remove with slotted spoon; drain on paper towels. Serve immediately.   Makes about 3 dozen

Estimated preparation time: 35 minutes
Cooking time: 10 minutes

Per 2 spinach ball serving: 87 calories, 3g protein, 5g fat (47% of calories), 9g carbohydrate, 25mg cholesterol, 205mg sodium, 1g dietary fiber

Hot Artichoke Cheese Dip

This mellow dip is a surefire crowd pleaser. Serve bread sticks as dippers.

1 can (14 ounces) PROGRESSO Artichoke Hearts, drained and finely chopped
1 jar (6 ounces) PROGRESSO Marinated Artichoke Hearts, undrained and finely chopped
¼ cup chopped PROGRESSO Tuscan Peppers (pepperoncini), stems and seeds removed before chopping
2 cups (8 ounces) shredded mozzarella cheese
¼ cup PROGRESSO Grated Parmesan Cheese
⅓ cup mayonnaise
½ teaspoon paprika

1. Preheat oven to 350°F.

2. In medium bowl, combine artichoke hearts, peppers, mozzarella cheese, Parmesan cheese and mayonnaise.

3. Spread into 9-inch pie plate; sprinkle with paprika. Cover.

4. Bake 15 to 20 minutes or until hot. Serve with bread sticks, fresh vegetable dippers or crackers.   Makes 8 appetizer servings

Estimated preparation time: 15 minutes
Baking time: 15 minutes

Per serving: 189 calories, 8g protein, 16g fat (72% of calories), 6g carbohydrate, 30mg cholesterol, 508mg sodium, 3g dietary fiber

Microwave Directions: Prepare artichoke mixture as directed above in Steps 2 and 3, *except* using 9-inch microwave-safe pie plate; cover. Microwave on HIGH (100% power) 6 minutes or until hot, turning every 2 minutes. Let stand 5 minutes before serving.

Seafood Dip-in-a-Round

A creamy dip that's easy to make and fun to serve. Your guests will love it!

1 sourdough bread round (about 1¼ pounds, 6½ inches in diameter)
1 can (10½ ounces) PROGRESSO White Clam Spaghetti Sauce
2 tablespoons all-purpose flour
2 tablespoons Dijon-style mustard
1 container (8 ounces) almond Swiss cold pack cheese food
⅓ cup chopped red bell pepper
1 tablespoon chopped green onion
2 tablespoons sliced almonds, toasted

1. Hollow out bread round to within 1-inch of crust. Cut removed bread into bite-size pieces.

2. In medium saucepan, heat white clam sauce, flour and mustard.

3. Add cheese spread, red pepper and onion; stir until smooth and thickened.

4. Fill bread shell with hot clam mixture; sprinkle with almonds. Dip bread pieces into hot clam mixture to serve.   Makes 10 appetizer servings

Estimated preparation time: 15 minutes
Cooking time: 5 minutes

Per serving: 267 calories, 13g protein, 10g fat (35% of calories), 30g carbohydrate, 21mg cholesterol, 685mg sodium, 1g dietary fiber

Microwave Directions: Cut bread as directed above in Step 1. In 1-quart microwave-safe casserole, combine white clam sauce, flour, mustard, cheese spread, red pepper and onion; cover. Microwave on HIGH (100% power) 1½ minutes or until hot and bubbly; stir. Microwave on MEDIUM (50% power) 2 minutes, stirring after each minute. Continue as directed above in Step 4.

Seafood Dip-in-a-Round

Vegetable Antipasto

Make your own spicy, marinated vegetables. Serve them as a light appetizer or salad.

2 cups cauliflower florets
1½ cups cubed zucchini
1½ cups cubed eggplant
1 cup thinly sliced carrots, cut on diagonal
1 cup thinly sliced celery, cut on diagonal
1 jar (9¾ ounces) PROGRESSO Olive Salad
1 jar (6 ounces) PROGRESSO Sweet Fried Peppers
2 tablespoons sugar
¼ teaspoon crushed red pepper
⅔ cup water
⅔ cup PROGRESSO Red Wine Vinegar
⅔ cup PROGRESSO Olive Oil

1. In 3-quart saucepan, combine all ingredients; mix well. Cover.

2. Cook over medium heat 4 to 6 minutes or until cauliflower is crisp-tender, stirring occasionally.

3. Remove from heat; uncover. Cool to room temperature, stirring occasionally.

4. Refrigerate overnight in glass or plastic covered container. (Keeps for 5 days in the refrigerator.) Arrange drained vegetables on platter to serve.

Makes 14 appetizer servings

Estimated preparation time: 20 minutes
Cooking time: 6 minutes
Chilling/cooling time: 8 hours

Per serving: 139 calories, 1g protein, 14g fat (81% of calories), 6g carbohydrate, 0mg cholesterol, 178mg sodium, 2g dietary fiber

Microwave Directions: In 3-quart microwave-safe casserole, combine all ingredients; mix well. Cover. Microwave on HIGH (100% power) 9 minutes or until cauliflower is crisp-tender, stirring every 4 minutes. Continue as directed above in Steps 3 and 4.

Zucchini Frittata

A simple Italian classic with the bright color of garden zucchini and roasted red peppers. So delicious and easy, you'll want to enjoy it often.

  6 eggs
  ⅓ cup PROGRESSO Grated Romano Cheese
  ⅓ cup chopped PROGRESSO Roasted Peppers (red)
  1 teaspoon dried basil leaves
  ¼ teaspoon salt
  ⅛ teaspoon ground black pepper
  3 tablespoons PROGRESSO Olive Oil
  ½ cup chopped zucchini
  ⅓ cup chopped onion

1. In medium bowl, beat eggs, Romano cheese, roasted peppers, basil, salt and black pepper until blended.

2. In large non-stick skillet, heat olive oil. Add zucchini and onion; cook 3 minutes or until tender, stirring occasionally.

3. Pour egg mixture over vegetables. Cook on low heat until egg mixture begins to set around outer edge. With spatula gently lift edge and tip skillet to allow uncooked egg to flow to bottom. Cook 4 minutes or until bottom is golden brown. Loosen edge with spatula; turn onto plate.

4. Return frittata to skillet, top side down. Cook 4 minutes or until bottom is golden brown. Cut into wedges to serve.

Makes 8 appetizer servings

Estimated preparation time: 20 minutes
Cooking time: 15 minutes

Per serving: 119 calories, 6g protein, 10g fat (74% of calories), 2g carbohydrate, 163mg cholesterol, 155mg sodium, ‹1g dietary fiber

Microwave Directions: In microwave-safe 10-inch quiche dish or pie plate, combine olive oil, zucchini and onion; cover. Microwave on HIGH (100% power) 2 minutes. In medium bowl, beat eggs, Romano cheese, roasted peppers, basil, salt and black pepper until blended; pour over vegetables. Microwave on MEDIUM (50% power) 6 minutes, stirring cooked portions toward center every 2 minutes. Continue microwaving 3 to 4 minutes or until almost set. Let stand 5 minutes before serving.

Soups & Breads

Roasted Red Pepper Biscuits

Roasted red peppers and a few seasonings transform boxed biscuit mix into a colorful Italian bread. You'll be glad you tried them!

2 cups buttermilk biscuit mix
½ cup **PROGRESSO Grated Parmesan Cheese**
1 teaspoon dried oregano leaves
⅛ teaspoon cayenne pepper
1 jar (7 ounces) **PROGRESSO Roasted Peppers (red), drained, patted dry on paper towel and chopped**
⅔ cup milk

1. Preheat oven to 425°F.

2. In medium bowl, stir together biscuit mix, Parmesan cheese, oregano and cayenne pepper.

3. Add roasted peppers and milk to biscuit mixture; stir just until moistened.

4. Drop dough by heaping tablespoonfuls, 2 inches apart, onto greased baking sheet.

5. Bake 12 to 14 minutes or until browned.   Makes 1 dozen

Estimated preparation time: 10 minutes
Baking time: 14 minutes

Per 1 biscuit serving: 111 calories, 4g protein, 4g fat (32% of calories), 16g carbohydrate, 3mg cholesterol, 340mg sodium, 1g dietary fiber

Roasted Red Pepper Biscuits

Lobsterman's Choice Stew

A spicy stew, chock-full of fish and vegetables, that takes only minutes to prepare.

1 can (10½ ounces) PROGRESSO Rock Lobster Spaghetti Sauce
1 tablespoon cornstarch
1 large tomato, chopped
1½ cups quartered zucchini slices
  1 cup corn
  ½ cup chopped onion
  ½ cup sliced celery
  1 clove garlic, minced
  1 teaspoon seafood seasoning
  1 bay leaf
  ⅛ teaspoon ground thyme
  ¼ pound white fish, cut into bite-size pieces
  ¼ pound coarsely chopped lobster meat (real or imitation)

1. In large saucepan, combine rock lobster sauce and cornstarch.

2. Stir in vegetables, garlic and seasonings.

3. Bring to a boil; simmer 10 minutes, stirring occasionally.

4. Add fish and lobster; return to a boil. Simmer 6 to 7 minutes or until fish and lobster are cooked. Remove bay leaf just before serving.

Makes 4 servings

Estimated preparation time: 15 minutes
Cooking time: 20 minutes

Per serving: 192 calories, 15g protein, 6g fat (27% of calories), 22g carbohydrate, 39mg cholesterol, 894mg sodium, 3g dietary fiber

Microwave Directions: In 3-quart microwave-safe casserole, combine rock lobster sauce and cornstarch. Stir in vegetables, garlic and seasonings; cover. Microwave on HIGH (100% power) 8 minutes, stirring after 4 minutes. Stir in fish and lobster; cover. Microwave on HIGH 4 minutes or until fish and lobster are cooked. Remove bay leaf just before serving.

Zucchini Cheese Muffins

If you enjoy a savory bread, you'll like these easy-to-prepare zucchini muffins.

1 cup all-purpose flour
¾ cup PROGRESSO Italian Style or Plain Bread Crumbs
¾ cup sugar
1½ teaspoons baking powder
1 teaspoon salt
1 cup (4 ounces) shredded Cheddar cheese
2 eggs, beaten
1 can (5 fluid ounces) PET Evaporated Milk
¼ cup butter, melted
1½ cups shredded zucchini

1. Preheat oven to 400° F.

2. In large bowl, combine flour, bread crumbs, sugar, baking powder and salt; stir in cheese.

3. In medium bowl, combine eggs, evaporated milk and butter; stir in zucchini.

4. Add zucchini mixture to flour mixture; stir just until moistened.

5. Spoon into greased muffin cups.

6. Bake 20 to 22 minutes or until lightly browned.   Makes 1½ dozen

Estimated preparation time: 10 minutes
Baking time: 22 minutes

Per 1 muffin serving: 147 calories, 4g protein, 6g fat (38% of calories), 19g carbohydrate, 39mg cholesterol, 305mg sodium, ‹1g dietary fiber

Cream of Chick Pea Soup

In Italy, chick peas are used in many ways—among them blended into velvety smooth soup. This one is accented with prosciutto. Chick peas are also called garbanzo beans.

1 can (15 ounces) PROGRESSO Chick Peas, drained
1 cup PET Evaporated Milk
2 tablespoons PROGRESSO Olive Oil
¼ cup diced prosciutto or ham
¼ cup chopped onion
⅛ teaspoon salt
⅛ teaspoon ground black pepper
4 teaspoons PROGRESSO Grated Parmesan Cheese

1. In blender or food processor, place chick peas; blend until smooth.

2. Blend in evaporated milk; set aside.

3. In large skillet, heat olive oil. Add prosciutto and onion; cook until onion is tender.

4. Stir in chick pea mixture, salt and pepper; heat thoroughly, stirring occasionally.

5. Top individual servings of soup with 1 teaspoon Parmesan cheese.

Makes 4 servings

Estimated preparation time: 10 minutes
Cooking time: 10 minutes

Per serving: 265 calories, 15g protein, 14g fat (43% of calories), 26g carbohydrate, 24mg cholesterol, 476mg sodium, 5g dietary fiber

Black Bean Soup

Canned beans streamline the preparation of this robust soup.

2 cups water
1 cup sliced carrot
½ cup chopped celery
2 cloves garlic, minced
3 tablespoons instant minced onion
1 teaspoon low sodium instant beef bouillon granules
1 teaspoon ground thyme
2 cans (15 ounces each) PROGRESSO Black Beans
¼ cup sherry, optional

1. In 4-quart Dutch oven, combine water, carrots, celery, garlic, onion, beef bouillon and thyme.

2. Bring to a boil. Reduce heat; cover. Simmer 15 minutes or until vegetables are tender.

3. Strain mixture, reserving broth and vegetables; return broth to Dutch oven.

4. In blender or food processor, place vegetables and beans; blend until smooth. Return bean mixture to broth. Add sherry; heat thoroughly, stirring occasionally.

Makes 6 servings

Estimated preparation time: 20 minutes
Cooking time: 20 minutes

Per serving: 142 calories, 11g protein, 1g fat (7% of calories), 28g carbohydrate, 0mg cholesterol, 436mg sodium, 9g dietary fiber

Italian Wedding Soup

The pasta adds a light, creamy body to the broth, and contrasts deliciously with the savory meatballs.

1 pound ground beef
1 cup PROGRESSO Italian Style Bread Crumbs
1 egg, lightly beaten
2 teaspoons Worcestershire sauce
1 teaspoon garlic powder
2 tablespoons PROGRESSO Olive Oil
5 cups chicken broth
1 cup water
1½ cups pastina or any miniature pasta
1 package (10 ounces) frozen chopped spinach, cooked according to package directions, drained

1. In large bowl, combine ground beef, bread crumbs, egg, Worcestershire sauce and garlic powder; mix well.

2. Shape meatballs using 1 rounded teaspoon meat mixture for each meatball.

3. In large skillet, heat olive oil. Add meatballs; cook 5 to 7 minutes or to desired doneness, turning occasionally to brown on all sides. Drain.

4. In large saucepan, bring chicken broth and water to a boil. Reduce heat. Add meatballs, pastina and spinach; cover. Simmer 10 minutes.

Makes 8 servings

Estimated preparation time: 30 minutes
Cooking time: 20 minutes

Per serving: 388 calories, 26g protein, 18g fat (43% of calories), 29g carbohydrate, 88mg cholesterol, 819mg sodium, 2g dietary fiber

Vegetables & Salads

Marinated Three Bean Salad

A colorful salad made from the simplest of ingredients—great company fare.

1 can (10½ ounces) PROGRESSO Red Kidney Beans, drained
1 can (10½ ounces) PROGRESSO Cannellini Beans, drained
1 can (10½ ounces) PROGRESSO Chick Peas, drained
1 medium green pepper, cut into matchstick strips
1 small onion, thinly sliced and separated into rings
½ cup sliced celery
⅓ cup halved carrot slices
¼ cup PROGRESSO Olive Oil
¼ cup PROGRESSO Red Wine Vinegar
2 tablespoons PROGRESSO Grated Parmesan Cheese
¾ teaspoon Italian seasoning
¼ teaspoon sugar

1. In large bowl, combine beans, chick peas and vegetables.

2. In small bowl, whisk together remaining ingredients; pour over bean mixture.

3. Refrigerate several hours or overnight.   Makes 8 servings

Estimated preparation time: 25 minutes
Chilling time: 3 hours

Per serving: 163 calories, 9g protein, 8g fat (39% of calories), 21g carbohydrate, 1mg cholesterol, 230mg sodium, 6g dietary fiber

Marinated Three Bean Salad

Tasty Bread Crumb Topping for Vegetables

A simple crunchy topping that adds the robust flavor of Southern Italy to any vegetable. Try it also on broiled chicken.

2 tablespoons PROGRESSO Olive Oil
⅓ cup finely chopped onion
1 clove garlic, minced
½ cup PROGRESSO Italian Style or Plain Bread Crumbs

1. In medium skillet, heat olive oil. Add onion and garlic; cook 3 minutes or until tender.

2. Add bread crumbs; cook 3 minutes, stirring occasionally.

3. Serve over hot cooked vegetables.
Makes 1 cup

Estimated preparation time: 5 minutes

Per 2 tablespoon serving: 63 calories, 1g protein, 4g fat (55% of calories), 6g carbohydrate, 0mg cholesterol, 120mg sodium, ‹1g dietary fiber

Mediterranean Pasta Salad

2 jars (6 ounces each) PROGRESSO Marinated Artichoke Hearts, undrained and cut into chunks
½ pound fusilli (corkscrew-shaped pasta), cooked according to package directions
½ cup PROGRESSO Italian Style Bread Crumbs
¼ cup PROGRESSO Grated Parmesan Cheese
⅓ cup chopped celery
⅓ cup chopped green pepper
1 medium tomato, cubed
¼ cup chopped red onion
1 tablespoon PROGRESSO Red Wine Vinegar

1. In large bowl, combine artichoke hearts, fusilli, bread crumbs, Parmesan cheese, celery, green pepper, tomato, red onion and vinegar; toss gently.

2. Refrigerate 1 hour.
Makes 4 servings

Estimated preparation time: 25 minutes
Chilling time: 1 hour

Per serving: 307 calories, 12g protein, 4g fat (12% of calories), 57g carbohydrate, 4mg cholesterol, 353mg sodium, 3g dietary fiber

Tasty Bread Crumb Topping
for Vegetables

Artichoke Spinach Salad

Fresh crisp spinach, slivers of red cabbage, artichoke hearts and strips of cheese and ham—a great combination of flavors and textures.

½ cup PROGRESSO Olive Oil
¼ cup PROGRESSO Red Wine Vinegar
 1 tablespoon lemon juice
 1 tablespoon Dijon-style mustard
½ teaspoon sugar
½ teaspoon salt
½ teaspoon dried dill weed
¼ teaspoon ground black pepper
 6 ounces (approximately 6 cups) fresh spinach, washed, trimmed and torn into bite-size pieces
 1 cup shredded red cabbage
 1 can (14 ounces) PROGRESSO Artichoke Hearts, drained and quartered
 4 ounces cooked ham, cut into thin strips
 4 ounces Muenster or provolone cheese, cut into thin strips

1. For dressing, whisk together olive oil, vinegar, lemon juice, mustard, sugar, salt, dill and pepper.

2. In large bowl, combine spinach, cabbage, artichoke hearts, ham and cheese.

3. Pour dressing over salad; toss gently.   Makes 4 entree servings

Estimated preparation time: 20 minutes

Per serving: 417 calories, 17g protein, 39g fat (80% of calories), 6g carbohydrate, 43mg cholesterol, 948mg sodium, 3g dietary fiber

Artichoke Spinach Salad

Eggplant Parmesan with Peppers

The Italians have long honored the humble eggplant in delicious creations. This tradition is streamlined with marinara sauce, grated Parmesan and jarred sweet fried peppers.

1 medium eggplant (about 1 pound)
1 teaspoon salt
1 egg, lightly beaten
⅓ cup PET Evaporated Milk
1 cup PROGRESSO Italian Style Bread Crumbs
2 tablespoons PROGRESSO Grated Parmesan Cheese, divided usage
¼ cup all-purpose flour
¼ cup PROGRESSO Olive Oil
1 jar (14 ounces) PROGRESSO Marinara Sauce
1 jar (6 ounces) PROGRESSO Sweet Fried Peppers, drained
1 cup (4 ounces) shredded mozzarella cheese

1. Slice eggplant into ½-inch slices; place in shallow pan. Sprinkle with salt. Refrigerate 30 minutes.

2. Preheat oven to 350°F.

3. In small bowl, combine egg and evaporated milk.

4. In small shallow dish, combine bread crumbs and 1 tablespoon Parmesan cheese.

5. Rinse eggplant slices; drain. Dip eggplant into flour, then into egg mixture. Coat with bread crumb mixture.

6. In large skillet, heat olive oil. Add eggplant; cook until browned on both sides. Drain on paper towel; place in 13×9-inch baking dish.

7. Top eggplant with marinara sauce, fried peppers, mozzarella cheese and remaining 1 tablespoon Parmesan cheese.

8. Bake 20 minutes or until thoroughly heated.   Makes 6 servings

Estimated preparation time: 35 minutes
Baking time: 20 minutes

Per serving: 350 calories, 13g protein, 21g fat (52% of calories), 32g carbohydrate, 56mg cholesterol, 729mg sodium, 4g dietary fiber

Italian Chicken Salad

A green salad tossed with a hot chicken dressing—a perfect luncheon dish.

  **1 can (19 ounces) PROGRESSO Minestrone Soup, drained, reserving
    broth and soup pieces separately**
1½ cups uncooked chicken strips
  2 tablespoons cornstarch
  2 tablespoons PROGRESSO Red Wine Vinegar
  2 tablespoons vegetable oil
  1 tablespoon prepared hot mustard
  1 teaspoon Italian seasoning
  ¼ teaspoon garlic salt
  ¼ teaspoon ground black pepper
  1 medium bunch romaine lettuce, torn (about 6 cups)
  ½ cup halved cherry tomatoes
  ½ cup sliced fresh mushrooms
  ¼ cup chopped green onions

1. In small bowl, pour half of reserved soup broth over chicken; cover. Refrigerate 2 hours.

2. In medium saucepan, cook chicken mixture over medium heat until chicken is no longer pink in center, stirring occasionally.

3. In small bowl, combine cornstarch and remaining reserved soup broth; stir until smooth. Stir in vinegar, oil, mustard, Italian seasoning, garlic salt and pepper.

4. Add broth mixture to chicken mixture; heat until thick and bubbly, stirring constantly.

5. In large bowl, combine lettuce, soup pieces, tomatoes, mushrooms and green onions.

6. Pour hot chicken mixture over salad; toss gently.   Makes 4 servings

Estimated preparation time: 20 minutes
Chilling/cooling time: 2 hours
Cooking time: 30 minutes

Per serving: 199 calories, 12g protein, 10g fat (41% of calories), 19g carbohydrate, 17mg cholesterol, 716mg sodium, 5g dietary fiber

Microwave Directions: In 1½-quart microwave-safe casserole, pour half of reserved soup broth over chicken; cover. Refrigerate 2 hours. Microwave on HIGH (100% power) 5 minutes or until chicken is no longer pink in center, stirring every 2 minutes. Continue as directed above in Step 3. Add broth mixture to chicken mixture. Microwave on HIGH 2 to 2½ minutes or until thoroughly heated, stirring after each minute. Continue as directed above in Steps 5 and 6.

Summer Bean Salad

A delicious high-fiber salad made from canned beans. Mandarin oranges add a surprising flavor touch.

½ cup **PROGRESSO Olive Oil**
¼ cup **PROGRESSO Red Wine Vinegar**
 1 **teaspoon sugar**
¼ **teaspoon ground black pepper, optional**
 2 **cans (11 ounces each) mandarin orange segments, drained**
 1 **can (19 ounces) PROGRESSO Chick Peas, drained**
 1 **can (19 ounces) PROGRESSO Red Kidney Beans, drained**
½ **medium red onion, cut into matchstick strips**
 1 **green pepper, cut into matchstick strips**
¼ **cup chopped fresh parsley**
   Lettuce leaves

1. For dressing, whisk together olive oil, vinegar, sugar and black pepper.

2. In large bowl, combine mandarin oranges, chick peas, beans, onion, green pepper and parsley.

3. Pour dressing over salad; toss gently.

4. Serve on lettuce leaves.   Makes 7 servings

Estimated preparation time: 20 minutes

Per serving: 314 calories, 12g protein, 17g fat (44% of calories), 38g carbohydrate, 0mg cholesterol, 272mg sodium, 10g dietary fiber

Summer Bean Salad

Asparagus with Roasted Peppers

This colorful salad—made easy with prepared roasted peppers—tastes as good as it looks.

16 asparagus spears
1 jar (7 ounces) PROGRESSO Roasted Peppers (red), drained and cut into strips
¼ cup PROGRESSO Olive Oil
4 teaspoons raspberry vinegar
⅛ teaspoon salt
Ground black pepper, to taste

1. Steam asparagus just until tender. Combine with roasted peppers; chill.

2. For dressing, whisk together remaining ingredients; chill.

3. When ready to serve, place asparagus on serving platter; top with roasted peppers, arranging in decorative design, if desired. Serve with dressing.

Makes 4 servings

Estimated preparation time: 10 minutes
Cooking time: 10 minutes
Chilling/cooling time: 2 hours

Per serving: 142 calories, 2g protein, 15g fat (82% of calories), 5g carbohydrate, 0mg cholesterol, 66mg sodium, 2g dietary fiber

Microwave Directions: In 1½-quart microwave-safe casserole, place asparagus and ¼ cup water; cover. Microwave on HIGH (100% power) 3 minutes or just until tender; drain. Add roasted peppers; chill. Continue as directed above in Steps 2 through 3.

Asparagus with Roasted Peppers

Pasta and Bean Salad

Convenient canned beans and artichoke hearts tossed with a tart Italian dressing make this an easy and tasty salad.

½ cup PROGRESSO Olive Oil
3 tablespoons PROGRESSO Red Wine Vinegar
¼ cup PROGRESSO Grated Parmesan Cheese
¾ teaspoon Italian seasoning
½ teaspoon salt
¼ teaspoon dry mustard
¼ teaspoon sugar
¼ teaspoon ground black pepper
⅛ teaspoon cayenne pepper
1 clove garlic, minced
½ pound ziti pasta, cooked according to package directions
1 can (10½ ounces) PROGRESSO Chick Peas, drained
1 can (10½ ounces) PROGRESSO Red Kidney Beans, drained
1 jar (6 ounces) PROGRESSO Marinated Artichoke Hearts, drained
   and cut into chunks
2 stalks celery, chopped
2 medium tomatoes, cut into wedges

1. For dressing, whisk together olive oil, vinegar, Parmesan cheese, Italian seasoning, salt, mustard, sugar, peppers and garlic.

2. In large bowl, combine remaining ingredients.

3. Pour dressing over salad; toss gently.

4. Refrigerate 2 hours or overnight.   Makes 8 servings

Estimated preparation time: 25 minutes
Chilling time: 2 hours

Per serving: 332 calories, 11g protein, 18g fat (45% of calories), 39g carbohydrate, 2mg cholesterol, 436mg sodium, 7g dietary fiber

Italian Garden Medley

Three of Italy's most popular vegetables are combined into an easy casserole and topped with crisp seasoned bread crumbs.

2 tablespoons PROGRESSO Olive Oil
4 cups thinly sliced zucchini, cut on diagonal (about 3 medium zucchini)
1 medium onion, sliced and separated into rings
3 medium tomatoes, coarsely chopped
1 cup (4 ounces) shredded mozzarella cheese
1 cup vegetable juice
1 teaspoon cornstarch
½ teaspoon salt
½ teaspoon garlic powder
¼ teaspoon ground black pepper
¼ cup PROGRESSO Italian Style Bread Crumbs

1. Preheat oven to 350°F.

2. In large skillet, heat olive oil. Add zucchini and onion; cook 4 minutes or until zucchini is crisp-tender, stirring occasionally.

3. In 2-quart casserole, combine zucchini mixture, tomatoes, cheese, juice, cornstarch, salt, garlic powder and pepper. Top with bread crumbs.

4. Bake 30 minutes or until thoroughly heated. Broil 2 to 3 minutes or until top is golden brown. Makes 6 servings

Estimated preparation time: 20 minutes
Baking time: 32 minutes

Per serving: 155 calories, 6g protein, 9g fat (52% of calories), 13g carbohydrate, 15mg cholesterol, 483mg sodium, 2g dietary fiber

Microwave Directions: Reduce vegetable juice to ¾ cup. In 2-quart microwave-safe casserole, combine olive oil, zucchini and onion; cover. Microwave on HIGH (100% power) 3 minutes. Stir in tomatoes, cheese, juice, cornstarch, salt, garlic powder and pepper; top with bread crumbs. Microwave on HIGH 8 to 9 minutes or until thoroughly heated, rotating dish after 5 minutes. If desired, place under broiler 2 to 3 minutes to brown top.

Pasta, Beans & Rice

Risotto

2 tablespoons PROGRESSO Olive Oil
1 small onion, sliced and quartered
½ pound fresh mushrooms, sliced
1 cup dry white wine
2 cans (16 ounces each) PROGRESSO Italian Style Zucchini,
   undrained
3 cups hot cooked rice
1 tablespoon dried basil leaves, optional

1. In large skillet, heat olive oil over medium heat. Add onion; cook until tender.

2. Stir in mushrooms and wine; cook 20 to 25 minutes or until wine is evaporated, stirring occasionally.

3. Stir in zucchini; bring to a boil.

4. Spoon rice onto serving platter; top with zucchini mixture. Sprinkle with basil.   Makes 6 servings

Estimated preparation time: 15 minutes
Cooking time: 30 minutes

Per serving: 279 calories, 5g protein, 8g fat (27% of calories), 42g carbohydrate, 1mg cholesterol, 725mg sodium, 4g dietary fiber

Microwave Directions: In 1½-quart microwave-safe casserole, combine olive oil and onion; cover. Microwave on HIGH (100% power) 2 minutes or until tender. Stir in mushrooms and wine. Microwave, uncovered, on HIGH 10 to 12 minutes or until wine is evaporated, stirring after 6 minutes. Stir in zucchini; cover. Microwave on HIGH 4 minutes or until mixture comes to a boil, stirring after 2 minutes. Continue as directed above in Step 4.

Risotto

Home-Style Spaghetti and Meatballs

Everyone's "Italian favorite" made easy with Progresso spaghetti sauce.

  1 pound ground beef
¾ cup PROGRESSO Italian Style Bread Crumbs, divided usage
½ cup water
½ cup chopped onion
¼ cup PROGRESSO Grated Parmesan Cheese
  1 egg, lightly beaten
  1 clove garlic, minced
⅛ teaspoon ground black pepper
¼ cup PROGRESSO Olive Oil
  1 jar (14 ounces) PROGRESSO Spaghetti Sauce
  8 ounces spaghetti, cooked according to package directions

1. In large bowl, combine ground beef, ¼ cup bread crumbs, water, onion, Parmesan cheese, egg, garlic and pepper.

2. Shape meatballs using ¼ cup meat mixture for each meatball; coat meatballs with remaining ½ cup bread crumbs.

3. In large skillet, heat olive oil. Add meatballs. Cook 5 to 7 minutes, turning occasionally to brown on all sides; drain.

4. Stir in spaghetti sauce; bring to a boil. Reduce heat; cover. Simmer 20 minutes, stirring occasionally. Serve over hot spaghetti.

Makes 4 servings

Estimated preparation time: 45 minutes
Cooking time: 30 minutes

Per serving: 785 calories, 45g protein, 47g fat (54% of calories), 46g carbohydrate, 181mg cholesterol, 1078mg sodium, 2g dietary fiber

Microwave Directions: Reduce olive oil to 2 tablespoons. Prepare meatballs as directed above in Steps 1 and 2. In 2-quart microwave-safe casserole, place meatballs in single layer. Drizzle olive oil over meatballs; cover. Microwave on HIGH (100% power) 8 minutes, turning meatballs after 4 minutes; drain. Pour spaghetti sauce over meatballs; cover. Microwave on MEDIUM (50% power) 10 minutes, stirring after 5 minutes. Serve over hot spaghetti.

Pasta e Fagioli
(Pasta and Beans)

A pasta with a hearty flavor and an unexpected ingredient—beans.
Complete the meal with a salad and crusty bread.

2 tablespoons PROGRESSO Olive Oil
½ cup chopped onion
⅓ cup chopped green pepper
⅓ cup chopped red bell pepper
¼ cup chopped celery
3 cloves garlic, minced
1 can (28 ounces) PROGRESSO Peeled Tomatoes Italian Style,
    undrained and chopped
1 teaspoon Italian seasoning
½ teaspoon dried basil leaves
¼ teaspoon salt
¼ teaspoon ground black pepper
1 cup ziti pasta, cooked according to package directions
1 can (15 ounces) PROGRESSO Cannellini Beans, drained
¼ cup PROGRESSO Grated Parmesan Cheese

1. In large skillet, heat olive oil. Add onion, green and red peppers, celery and garlic; cook 6 to 8 minutes or until tender, stirring occasionally.

2. Stir in tomatoes and seasonings; simmer 20 minutes, stirring occasionally.

3. Add pasta and beans; heat thoroughly, stirring occasionally.

4. Stir in Parmesan cheese.   Makes 4 servings

Estimated preparation time: 25 minutes
Cooking time: 25 minutes

Per serving: 307 calories, 15g protein, 11g fat (27% of calories), 50g carbohydrate, 4mg cholesterol, 754mg sodium, 10g dietary fiber

Microwave Directions: In 2-quart microwave-safe casserole, combine olive oil, onion, green and red peppers, celery and garlic; cover. Microwave on HIGH (100% power) 5 minutes, stirring every 2 minutes. Stir in tomatoes and seasonings; cover. Microwave on HIGH 15 minutes, stirring every 6 minutes. Stir in pasta and beans. Microwave on HIGH 3 minutes. Stir in Parmesan cheese.

Easy Family Lasagna

A simple way to prepare a favorite. The noodles are not precooked.

½ **pound bulk Italian sausage or ground turkey**
½ **cup chopped onion**
1 **can (28 ounces) PROGRESSO Peeled Tomatoes Italian Style,**
   undrained and chopped
1 **jar (14 ounces) PROGRESSO Spaghetti Sauce**
2 **teaspoons Italian seasoning**
9 **lasagna noodles, uncooked**
1 **container (15 ounces) ricotta cheese**
3 **cups (12 ounces) shredded mozzarella cheese**
¼ **cup PROGRESSO Grated Parmesan Cheese**

1. In medium skillet, brown sausage and onion; drain.

2. Stir in tomatoes, spaghetti sauce and Italian seasoning.

3. In lightly greased 12×8-inch baking dish, layer one third each of the lasagna noodles, ricotta cheese, meat mixture, mozzarella cheese and Parmesan cheese; repeat layers two more times. Cover.

4. Refrigerate at least 8 hours or up to 24 hours.

5. When ready to bake, remove cover; place in cold oven. Turn oven on to 350°F. Bake 45 to 50 minutes or until bubbly and cheese is lightly browned. Let stand 15 minutes before serving.   Makes 8 servings

Estimated preparation time: 20 minutes
Chilling/cooling time: 8 hours
Baking time: 50 minutes

Per serving: 462 calories, 27g protein, 24g fat (47% of calories), 35g carbohydrate, 75mg cholesterol, 981mg sodium, 2g dietary fiber

Microwave Directions: Crumble sausage into medium microwave-safe container; cover. Microwave on HIGH (100% power) 4 minutes, stirring and breaking sausage into small pieces after 2 minutes. Stir in onion. Microwave on HIGH 2 minutes; drain. Break up any remaining large pieces of sausage. Continue as directed above in Steps 2 through 4, *except* drain tomatoes, use 12×8-inch microwave-safe baking dish and cover dish with plastic wrap. When ready to microwave, cut a few slits in center of plastic wrap to vent. Microwave on HIGH 10 minutes, rotating dish after 5 minutes. Microwave on MEDIUM (50% power) 25 minutes or until bubbly, rotating dish every 5 minutes. Let stand 5 minutes before serving.

Variation:
Stir 1 package (10 ounces) frozen chopped spinach, thawed and well drained, into the ricotta cheese.

Easy Family Lasagna

Herbed Seafood Linguine

A light, colorful, easy-to-prepare pasta for seafood lovers.

1 can (10½ ounces) PROGRESSO Red Clam Spaghetti Sauce
¼ pound sole, cut into small pieces
3 ounces (about ½ cup) imitation crabmeat
2 ounces (8 to 10) peeled and deveined uncooked medium shrimp
⅓ cup chopped onion
¼ cup chopped green pepper
1 clove garlic, minced
⅛ teaspoon dried basil leaves
⅛ teaspoon dried oregano leaves
6 ounces linguine, cooked according to package directions
2 tablespoons PROGRESSO Grated Parmesan Cheese

1. In medium saucepan, combine red clam sauce, sole, crabmeat, shrimp, onion, green pepper, garlic, basil and oregano.

2. Bring to a boil; simmer until sole flakes easily with fork and shrimp turn pink.

3. Serve clam sauce mixture over linguine; sprinkle with Parmesan cheese.

Makes 4 servings

Estimated preparation time: 10 minutes
Cooking time: 10 minutes

Per serving: 282 calories, 22g protein, 4g fat (14% of calories), 38g carbohydrate, 56mg cholesterol, 509mg sodium, 2g dietary fiber

Microwave Directions: In 2-quart microwave-safe casserole, combine red clam sauce, sole, crabmeat, shrimp, onion, green pepper, garlic, basil and oregano; cover. Microwave on HIGH (100% power) 4 to 5 minutes or until sole flakes easily with fork and shrimp turn pink, stirring after 2 minutes. Serve over linguine; sprinkle with Parmesan cheese.

Easy Linguine Tutto Mare

A very easy seafood pasta prepared from on-hand ingredients.

1 jar (12 ounces) PROGRESSO White Clam Sauce
1 can (6 ounces) lump crabmeat, rinsed and drained
1 can (4¼ ounces) deveined medium shrimp, rinsed and drained
½ pound (8 ounces) linguine, cooked according to package directions

1. In small saucepan over medium heat, bring white clam sauce, crabmeat and shrimp just to a boil.

2. Add clam sauce mixture to linguine. If necessary, add 2 tablespoons water for desired consistency; toss gently. Serve immediately.

Makes 4 servings

Estimated preparation time: 15 minutes

Per serving: 365 calories, 29g protein, 8g fat (19% of calories) 43g carbohydrate, 90mg cholesterol, 392mg sodium, 2g dietary fiber

Microwave Directions: In 1-quart microwave-safe casserole, combine clam sauce, crabmeat and shrimp. Microwave on HIGH (100% power) 4½ to 5 minutes or until hot, stirring every 2 minutes. Continue as directed above in Step 2.

Black Beans and Rice

Beans and rice go nicely together. These black beans are further enhanced with herbs and ham.

2 tablespoons PROGRESSO Olive Oil
½ cup chopped onion
⅓ cup chopped celery
2 cloves garlic, minced
1 can (15 ounces) PROGRESSO Black Beans
⅓ cup coarsely chopped ham
½ teaspoon dried basil leaves
½ teaspoon dried oregano leaves
¼ teaspoon ground black pepper
3 to 5 drops hot pepper sauce
1½ cups hot cooked rice

1. In large skillet, heat olive oil. Add onion, celery and garlic; cook 5 minutes or until tender, stirring occasionally.

2. Add beans, ham, basil, oregano, black pepper and pepper sauce; simmer 8 minutes, stirring occasionally.

3. Serve over hot cooked rice.

Makes 4 servings

Estimated preparation time: 10 minutes
Cooking time: 15 minutes

Per serving: 266 calories, 13g protein, 9g fat (27% of calories), 41g carbohydrate, 6mg cholesterol, 494mg sodium, 7g dietary fiber

Microwave Directions: In 1½-quart microwave-safe casserole, combine olive oil, onion, celery and garlic; cover. Microwave on HIGH (100% power) 3 minutes. Stir in beans, ham, basil, oregano, black pepper and pepper sauce; cover. Microwave on HIGH 4 to 5 minutes or until hot and bubbly, stirring after 2½ minutes. Serve over hot cooked rice.

Chicken and Spinach Manicotti

Manicotti filled with the earthy flavors of Italy is baked as a casserole. A pastry bag with a large plain tip is an easy way to stuff manicotti.

1½ cups shredded cooked chicken
 1 container (15 ounces) ricotta cheese
 1 package (10 ounces) frozen chopped spinach, cooked according to
   package directions and well drained
1¼ cups half and half, divided usage
 ½ cup PROGRESSO Plain Bread Crumbs
 1 teaspoon garlic powder
 ½ teaspoon dried basil leaves
 ½ teaspoon dried oregano leaves
 ½ teaspoon salt
 ¼ teaspoon ground black pepper
 1 package (8 ounces; 14 count) manicotti noodles, cooked according to
   package directions
 1 jar (14 ounces) PROGRESSO Marinara Sauce
1½ cups (6 ounces) shredded mozzarella cheese

1. Preheat oven to 350°F.

2. In large bowl, combine chicken, ricotta cheese, spinach, ½ cup half and half, bread crumbs, garlic powder, basil, oregano, salt and pepper; mix well.

3. Stuff chicken mixture into manicotti; place in 13×9-inch baking dish.

4. Combine marinara sauce and remaining ¾ cup half and half; pour over manicotti. Top with mozzarella cheese.

5. Bake 30 minutes or until thoroughly heated.   Makes 7 servings

Estimated preparation time: 30 minutes
Baking time: 30 minutes

Per serving: 457 calories, 29g protein, 19g fat (38% of calories), 43g carbohydrate, 75mg cholesterol, 688mg sodium, 3g dietary fiber

Microwave Directions: Prepare chicken mixture and fill manicotti as directed above in Steps 2 and 3. Place in 13×9-inch microwave-safe baking dish. Combine marinara sauce and remaining ¾ cup half and half; pour over manicotti. Cover with plastic wrap, cutting a few slits in center of wrap to vent. Microwave on HIGH (100% power) 5 minutes; top with mozzarella cheese. Microwave on MEDIUM (50% power) 15 minutes, rotating dish every 5 minutes. Let stand 5 minutes before serving.

Chicken and Spinach Manicotti

Fettuccine with Mussels

If fresh mussels aren't available in your store, use canned clams.

1 can (10½ ounces) PROGRESSO White Clam Spaghetti Sauce
½ pound mussels in shells, cleaned
¼ cup PROGRESSO Grated Parmesan Cheese, divided usage
¼ teaspoon seafood seasoning
¼ teaspoon Italian seasoning
4 ounces spinach fettuccine, cooked according to package directions

1. In medium saucepan, combine white clam sauce, mussels, 2 tablespoons Parmesan cheese and seasonings. Bring to a boil over medium heat until mussels pop open. (Discard any mussels that remain closed.)

2. Serve clam sauce mixture over hot fettuccine. Sprinkle with remaining 2 tablespoons Parmesan cheese.

Makes 4 servings

Estimated preparation time: 15 minutes
Cooking time: 10 minutes

Per serving: 244 calories, 18g protein, 9g fat (31% of calories), 25g carbohydrate, 20mg cholesterol, 783mg sodium, 1g dietary fiber

Garden Pasta and Beans

2 tablespoons PROGRESSO Olive Oil
2 cloves garlic, minced
1½ cups cubed zucchini
1 cup chopped celery
1 can (28 ounces) PROGRESSO Peeled Tomatoes Italian Style, undrained and chopped
¾ cup (3 ounces) small shell pasta, cooked according to package directions
1 can (19 ounces) PROGRESSO Cannellini Beans
½ cup PROGRESSO Grated Parmesan Cheese

1. In large skillet, heat olive oil. Add garlic; cook 30 seconds. Add zucchini and celery; cook 5 minutes, stirring occasionally.

2. Add tomatoes; simmer 10 minutes, stirring occasionally.

3. Add pasta and beans; heat thoroughly, stirring occasionally; stir in Parmesan cheese.

Makes 4 servings

Estimated preparation time: 25 minutes

Per serving: 303 calories, 16g protein, 11g fat (27% of calories), 49g carbohydrate, 4mg cholesterol, 691mg sodium, 11g dietary fiber

Fettuccine with Mussels

Baked Pasta Parmesan

If your family likes the flavor of spaghetti, they'll like this easy pasta casserole.

1 tablespoon PROGRESSO Olive Oil
1 pound ground beef
1 can (19 ounces) PROGRESSO Minestrone Soup
1 can (8 ounces) PROGRESSO Tomato Sauce
1½ teaspoons dried basil leaves
½ teaspoon dried oregano leaves
⅛ teaspoon ground black pepper
1½ cups (6 ounces) rigatoni pasta, cooked according to package
    directions
½ cup PROGRESSO Grated Parmesan Cheese, divided usage
1 cup (4 ounces) shredded mozzarella cheese

1. Preheat oven to 375°F.

2. In large skillet, heat olive oil. Add ground beef; brown. Drain.

3. Add soup, tomato sauce, basil, oregano and pepper. Simmer 10 minutes
   or until slightly thickened, stirring occasionally.

4. In 8-inch square baking dish, spoon thin layer of meat mixture. Top with
   layers of pasta and remaining meat mixture.

5. Add layers of ¼ cup Parmesan cheese and mozzarella cheese; top with
   remaining ¼ cup Parmesan cheese.

6. Bake 25 minutes or until cheese is golden brown.   Makes 4 servings

Estimated preparation time: 20 minutes
Baking time: 25 minutes

Per serving: 756 calories, 52g protein, 41g fat (47% of calories), 50g carbohydrate,
153mg cholesterol, 1231mg sodium, 6g dietary fiber

Microwave Directions: In 1½-quart microwave-safe casserole, combine
olive oil and ground beef. Microwave on HIGH (100% power) 5 minutes,
stirring and breaking ground beef into small pieces after 2 minutes; drain.
Break up any remaining large pieces of ground beef. Stir in soup, tomato
sauce, basil, oregano and pepper. Microwave on HIGH 4 minutes, stirring
after 2 minutes. Microwave on MEDIUM (50% power) 10 minutes, stirring
every 3 minutes. Continue as directed above in Steps 4 and 5, *except* using
8-inch square microwave-safe baking dish. Microwave on HIGH 3 minutes
or until cheese is melted and mixture is thoroughly heated.

Lentíl Lasagna

This all-vegetable lasagna has a creamy texture and the slightly "nut-like" flavor of lentils.

1 tablespoon PROGRESSO Olive Oil
½ cup chopped onion
2 cloves garlic, minced
1 can (19 ounces) PROGRESSO Lentil Soup
1 can (8 ounces) PROGRESSO Tomato Sauce
1 can (6 ounces) PROGRESSO Tomato Paste
2 teaspoons Italian seasoning
9 lasagna noodles, cooked according to package directions
1 container (15 ounces) ricotta cheese
1 package (12 ounces) mozzarella cheese slices
¼ cup PROGRESSO Grated Parmesan Cheese

1. Preheat oven to 350°F.

2. In medium skillet, heat olive oil. Add onion and garlic; cook 2 to 3 minutes or until tender, stirring occasionally.

3. Add soup, tomato sauce, tomato paste and Italian seasoning; cook 10 minutes, stirring occasionally.

4. In greased 12×8-inch baking dish, layer one third each of the lasagna noodles, ricotta cheese, mozzarella cheese, soup mixture and Parmesan cheese; repeat layers two more times. Cover with foil.

5. Bake 35 to 40 minutes or until bubbly. Let stand 15 minutes before serving.   Makes 8 servings

Estimated preparation time: 30 minutes
Baking time: 40 minutes

Per serving: 379 calories, 25g protein, 15g fat (35% of calories), 39g carbohydrate, 43mg cholesterol, 863mg sodium, 4g dietary fiber

Microwave Directions: In small microwave-safe container, combine olive oil, onion and garlic; cover. Microwave on HIGH (100% power) 1 to 2 minutes or until tender. Stir in soup, tomato sauce, tomato paste and Italian seasoning; cover. Microwave on HIGH 3 minutes or until hot and bubbly, stirring after 2 minutes. Continue as directed above in Step 4, *except* using 12×8-inch microwave-safe baking dish and covering with plastic wrap; cut a few slits in center of wrap to vent. Microwave on HIGH 5 minutes; rotate dish. Microwave on MEDIUM (50% power) 20 minutes or until bubbly, rotating dish after 10 minutes. Let stand 5 minutes before serving.

Poultry Dishes

Pollo Pignoli
(Chicken with Pine Nuts)

½ cup **PROGRESSO Grated Parmesan Cheese**
½ cup **PROGRESSO Plain Bread Crumbs**
4 boneless, skinless chicken breast halves
Salt and ground black pepper
2 eggs, lightly beaten
1 tablespoon PROGRESSO Olive Oil
2 jars (7 ounces each) PROGRESSO Roasted Peppers (red), drained
and sliced into strips
⅓ cup **PROGRESSO Imported Pignoli (pine nuts)**

1. Preheat oven to 375°F.

2. In shallow dish, combine Parmesan cheese and bread crumbs.

3. Season chicken with salt and black pepper.

4. Dip chicken into eggs; coat with cheese mixture. Place chicken on lightly greased baking sheet.

5. Bake 20 to 25 minutes or until chicken is no longer pink in center. Keep warm.

6. In small skillet, heat olive oil over medium heat. Add roasted peppers and pine nuts. Cook until pine nuts begin to brown, stirring frequently; drain. Serve over chicken.

Makes 4 servings

Estimated preparation time: 15 minutes
Baking time: 20 minutes

Per serving: 391 calories, 41g protein, 20g fat (43% of calories), 17g carbohydrate, 182mg cholesterol, 473mg sodium, 1g dietary fiber

Pollo Pignoli

Pollo alla Giardiniera
(Gardener's Style Chicken)

Crisp fried chicken strips add a crunchy touch to this tossed salad.

⅓ cup all-purpose flour
⅛ teaspoon salt
⅛ teaspoon ground black pepper
4 boneless, skinless chicken breast halves
2 eggs, lightly beaten
¾ cup PROGRESSO Italian Style Bread Crumbs
½ cup butter
6 tablespoons PROGRESSO Olive Oil, divided usage
2 cups torn radicchio
2 cups torn romaine lettuce
1 cup chopped tomatoes
¼ cup PROGRESSO Red Wine Vinegar

1. In shallow dish or pie plate, combine flour, salt and pepper.

2. Roll chicken in flour mixture; dip into eggs. Coat with bread crumbs.

3. In large skillet, heat butter and 2 tablespoons olive oil over medium heat. Add chicken; cook 10 minutes or until browned on both sides and no longer pink in center.

4. Remove chicken from skillet; cut into strips.

5. In large bowl, combine radicchio and lettuce; top with tomatoes and chicken.

6. In small bowl, whisk together remaining ¼ cup olive oil and vinegar; pour over salad. Toss gently.   Makes 4 servings

Estimated preparation time: 25 minutes

Per serving: 712 calories, 37g protein, 50g fat (62% of calories), 32g carbohydrate, 236mg cholesterol, 827mg sodium, 3g dietary fiber

Pollo alla Giardiniera

Home Style Chicken Roll-Ups

This surprisingly easy chicken makes a tasty family meal.

2 tablespoons PROGRESSO Olive Oil
½ cup sliced mushrooms
1 small onion, chopped
¼ cup chopped green pepper
¼ cup PROGRESSO Italian Style Bread Crumbs
1 pound boneless, skinless chicken breast halves, pounded to ¼-inch
  thickness
1 can (19 ounces) PROGRESSO Home Style Chicken Soup

1. In 10-inch skillet, heat olive oil. Add mushrooms, onion and green pepper; cook 3 minutes or until tender, stirring occasionally. Remove from heat; stir in bread crumbs.

2. Place equal amounts of vegetable mixture on each chicken piece; roll, starting at short end. Secure with toothpicks.

3. Place chicken in skillet; cover with soup. Cook 15 minutes; cover. Continue cooking 10 to 15 minutes or until chicken is no longer pink in center. Remove toothpicks before serving.   Makes 4 servings

Estimated preparation time: 25 minutes
Cooking time: 30 minutes

Per serving: 280 calories, 33g protein, 10g fat (33% of calories), 14g carbohydrate, 76mg cholesterol, 564mg sodium, ‹1g dietary fiber

Chicken-in-a-Garden

Quick, light and tasty. If you have leftover vegetables, such as broccoli or asparagus, add them, too.

⅓ cup all-purpose flour
1 tablespoon chopped fresh parsley
1½ teaspoons dried basil leaves
1½ cups uncooked chicken strips
2 tablespoons PROGRESSO Olive Oil
1 clove garlic, minced
1 can (19 ounces) PROGRESSO Vegetable Soup
¾ cup halved cherry tomatoes
½ cup sliced mushrooms
½ cup diagonally sliced green onions
½ cup sliced zucchini

1. In small bowl, combine flour, parsley and basil.

2. Coat chicken with flour mixture.

3. In large skillet, heat olive oil. Add garlic; cook 1 minute.

4. Add chicken; cook until browned and no longer pink in center, stirring occasionally.

5. Add remaining ingredients; heat thoroughly, stirring frequently.

Makes 4 servings

Estimated preparation time: 10 minutes
Cooking time: 20 minutes

Per serving: 217 calories, 17g protein, 9g fat (36% of calories), 19g carbohydrate, 35mg cholesterol, 638mg sodium, 3g dietary fiber

Italian Country Chicken

This quick-to-prepare dish with a lively flavor is great for after work.

4 boneless, skinless chicken breast halves
3 tablespoons PROGRESSO Italian Style Bread Crumbs
2 tablespoons PROGRESSO Olive Oil
1 can (19 ounces) PROGRESSO Minestrone Soup
2 tablespoons PROGRESSO Red Wine Vinegar
⅛ teaspoon sugar
1 can (14 ounces) PROGRESSO Artichoke Hearts, drained and halved
½ cup chopped fresh parsley
Cooked pasta, optional

1. Lightly coat chicken on both sides with bread crumbs.

2. In large skillet, heat olive oil over medium heat. Add chicken; cook 15 minutes or until browned on both sides and no longer pink in center.

3. In small bowl, combine soup, vinegar and sugar. Pour over chicken; cover. Simmer 5 minutes.

4. Stir in artichoke hearts and parsley; heat thoroughly. Serve over hot pasta, if desired.

Makes 4 servings

Estimated preparation time: 10 minutes
Cooking time: 25 minutes

Per serving (without pasta): 279 calories, 32g protein, 11g fat (34% of calories), 16g carbohydrate, 68mg cholesterol, 679mg sodium, 3g dietary fiber

Northern Italian Chicken and Mushrooms

An easy, tasty main dish that's ideal for an after-work family meal.

3 tablespoons PROGRESSO Olive Oil
1 pound boneless, skinless chicken breast halves
1 cup sliced mushrooms
1 small onion, sliced and separated into rings
1 can (19 ounces) PROGRESSO Chicken Vegetable Soup
½ cup sour cream
2 teaspoons cornstarch
2 cups egg noodles, cooked according to package directions

1. In large skillet, heat olive oil over medium heat. Add chicken; cook 15 minutes or until browned on both sides and chicken is no longer pink in center.

2. Remove chicken from skillet, reserving oil in skillet. Add mushrooms and onions to skillet; cook 5 minutes or until tender. (Add additional oil, if necessary.)

3. Return chicken to skillet. Pour soup over chicken; cover. Simmer 5 minutes.

4. Stir sour cream and cornstarch into soup mixture, rearranging chicken as necessary. Heat thoroughly until soup mixture is thickened, stirring occasionally.

5. Serve over hot noodles.   Makes 4 servings

Estimated preparation time: 15 minutes
Cooking time: 30 minutes

Per serving: 466 calories, 36g protein, 21g fat (41% of calories), 33g carbohydrate, 117mg cholesterol, 495mg sodium, 2g dietary fiber

Microwave Directions: Reduce olive oil to 1 tablespoon. In 1½-quart microwave-safe casserole, pour 1 tablespoon olive oil, tilting casserole to evenly coat bottom. Place chicken in single layer in casserole, turning to coat with oil; cover. Microwave on HIGH (100% power) 5 minutes or until chicken is no longer pink in center, turning chicken over after 2½ minutes. Stir in mushrooms and onions; cover. Microwave on HIGH 1 minute. Stir in soup; cover. Microwave on HIGH 5 minutes, stirring after 3 minutes. In small dish, combine sour cream and cornstarch; stir into soup mixture. Cover. Microwave on MEDIUM (50% power) 5 minutes or until soup mixture is thickened, stirring after 3 minutes. Serve over hot noodles.

Northern Italian Chicken and
Mushrooms

Tangy Chicken Vegetable Bake

This easy casserole has the fresh taste of a hot chicken salad.

¾ **cup mayonnaise**
¼ **cup sour cream**
3 **tablespoons butter, melted**
3 **tablespoons lemon juice**
1 **teaspoon dry mustard**
⅛ **teaspoon ground black pepper**
1 **package (16 ounces) frozen broccoli, cauliflower and carrots, thawed**
½ **cup sliced fresh mushrooms**
2 **cups chopped cooked chicken (about 1 pound uncooked)**
¾ **cup (3 ounces) shredded Monterey Jack cheese**
⅓ **cup PROGRESSO Italian Style Bread Crumbs**

1. Preheat oven to 375°F.

2. In medium bowl, combine mayonnaise, sour cream, butter, lemon juice, mustard and pepper.

3. In 2-quart casserole, combine vegetables and chicken. Stir in mayonnaise mixture.

4. Bake 15 minutes or until thoroughly heated.

5. Sprinkle with cheese and bread crumbs.

6. Broil, 8 to 10 inches from heat source, until bread crumbs are lightly browned.   Makes 4 servings

Estimated preparation time: 15 minutes
Baking time: 18 minutes

Per serving: 692 calories, 30g protein, 57g fat (73% of calories), 17g carbohydrate, 135mg cholesterol, 616mg sodium, 4g dietary fiber

Microwave Directions: Prepare mayonnaise mixture as directed above in Step 2. In shallow 2-quart microwave-safe baking dish, combine vegetables and chicken. Stir in mayonnaise mixture; cover. Microwave on HIGH (100% power) 4 minutes, rotating dish after 2 minutes; sprinkle with cheese and bread crumbs. Microwave on HIGH 45 seconds *OR* broil as directed above in Step 6.

Tangy Chicken Vegetable Bake

Coconut Chicken

*For special occasions, try this crisp, coconutty chicken in a
velvety-smooth red pepper sauce.*

⅔ cup **PROGRESSO Italian Style Bread Crumbs**
⅔ cup **shredded coconut**
 1 pound **boneless, skinless chicken breast halves, pounded to ¼-inch
  thickness**
 2 **eggs, lightly beaten**
¼ cup **PROGRESSO Olive Oil, divided usage**
¼ cup **sliced green onions**
 2 **cloves garlic, minced**
 1 cup **PET Evaporated Milk**
 1 jar (7 ounces) **PROGRESSO Roasted Peppers (red), drained and
  pureed**
 1 teaspoon **dried basil leaves**

1. In small bowl, combine bread crumbs and coconut.

2. Dip chicken into egg; coat with bread crumb mixture.

3. In large skillet, heat 3 tablespoons olive oil. Add chicken; cook 5 to
   7 minutes or until browned on both sides and no longer pink in center.
   Cover; set aside to keep warm.

4. In small skillet, heat remaining 1 tablespoon olive oil. Add green onions
   and garlic; cook 1 minute.

5. Add evaporated milk, peppers and basil; simmer 3 minutes, stirring
   constantly. To serve, spoon roasted pepper mixture onto serving plates;
   top with chicken.   Makes 4 servings

Estimated preparation time: 30 minutes
Cooking time: 15 minutes

Per serving: 538 calories, 37g protein, 30g fat (50% of calories), 32g carbohydrate,
190mg cholesterol, 538mg sodium, 4g dietary fiber

Tuscan Valley Chicken Breasts

A "special occasion" entree that's well worth the time. The stuffing is an exciting blend of flavors and colors, making the final dish extraordinary.

1 can (14 ounces) PROGRESSO Artichoke Hearts, drained and
   coarsely chopped
1 jar (7 ounces) PROGRESSO Roasted Peppers (red), drained and
   coarsely chopped
1 jar (6 ounces) PROGRESSO Marinated Mushrooms, drained and
   coarsely chopped
1 cup PROGRESSO Italian Style Bread Crumbs
1 teaspoon dried oregano leaves
⅛ teaspoon salt
⅛ teaspoon ground black pepper
12 boneless, skinless chicken breast halves, pounded to ¼-inch
   thickness
4 slices bacon, chopped
1 medium onion, chopped
1 can (10½ ounces) PROGRESSO Lentil Soup, pureed
½ cup dry white wine
1 can (16 ounces) PROGRESSO Peeled Tomatoes Italian Style,
   drained and chopped
2 tablespoons sliced green onion
1 tablespoon butter

1. Preheat oven to 375°F.

2. In large bowl, combine artichoke hearts, roasted peppers, mushrooms, bread crumbs, oregano, salt and black pepper; mix well.

3. Place approximately ⅓ cup artichoke mixture in center of each chicken breast; roll, starting at short end. Secure with toothpicks. Place in large shallow baking dish.

4. Bake 30 minutes or until chicken is no longer pink in center; remove toothpicks. Keep warm.

5. In small skillet, cook bacon 2 minutes. Add onion. Continue cooking until bacon is crisp, stirring occasionally; drain. Stir in soup and wine; simmer 5 minutes. Add tomatoes, green onion and butter; simmer 10 minutes, stirring occasionally. Serve over chicken.

Makes 6 servings

Estimated preparation time: 1 hour
Baking time: 30 minutes

Per serving: 540 calories, 64g protein, 18g fat (31% of calories), 30g carbohydrate, 146mg cholesterol, 1267mg sodium, 7g dietary fiber

Chicken Saltimbocca

Chicken replaces veal in this popular Italian dish. It's so good that the name literally means "leap into the mouth."

4 boneless, skinless chicken breast halves, pounded to ¼-inch thickness
4 slices (1 ounce each) ham
4 slices (½ ounce each) Swiss cheese
2 eggs, lightly beaten
¾ cup PROGRESSO Italian Style Bread Crumbs
5 tablespoons PROGRESSO Olive Oil, divided usage
¼ cup sliced green onions
1 clove garlic, minced
1 tablespoon all-purpose flour
⅓ cup chicken broth
¼ cup dry white wine

1. Preheat oven to 350°F.

2. Top each chicken breast with 1 slice of ham and cheese. (If necessary, fold ham and cheese slices in half to fit onto top of each chicken piece.) Roll each chicken breast, starting at short end; secure with toothpicks.

3. Dip chicken into egg; coat with bread crumbs.

4. In large skillet, heat 3 tablespoons olive oil. Add chicken; cook 5 to 7 minutes or until browned on both sides.

5. Place chicken in lightly greased 8-inch square baking dish.

6. Bake 20 minutes or until chicken is no longer pink in center; remove toothpicks. Keep warm.

7. In large skillet, heat remaining 2 tablespoons olive oil. Add onions and garlic; cook 2 minutes or until tender, stirring occasionally. Stir in flour. Gradually stir in chicken broth and wine; bring to a boil. Serve over chicken.

Makes 4 servings

Estimated preparation time: 25 minutes
Baking time: 20 minutes

Per serving: 531 calories, 43g protein, 30g fat (51% of calories), 21g carbohydrate, 204mg cholesterol, 946mg sodium, 1g dietary fiber

Chicken Saltimbocca

Meat Dishes

Fillet of Beef Andrea

A sprightly sauce of garlic, olives and chick peas complements beef.

5 tablespoons PROGRESSO Olive Oil, divided usage
4 tablespoons PROGRESSO Red Wine Vinegar, divided usage
¾ teaspoon PROGRESSO Garlic Puree, divided usage
4 (1½-inch thick) beef fillets or strip steaks (about ½ to ¾ pound each)
1 can (19 ounces) PROGRESSO Chick Peas, drained
¾ cup sliced ripe olives

1. In small bowl, combine 2 tablespoons olive oil, 2 tablespoons wine vinegar and ¼ teaspoon garlic puree.

2. Place beef fillets in glass baking dish. Pour olive oil mixture over fillets; cover. Refrigerate 2 hours, turning frequently.

3. In hot 12-inch skillet, cook fillets on both sides to desired doneness. Remove from skillet; keep warm.

4. Add remaining 3 tablespoons olive oil, 2 tablespoons wine vinegar and ½ teaspoon garlic puree to skillet; simmer 3 minutes, stirring occasionally.

5. Stir in chick peas and olives; simmer 1 minute. Serve over fillets.

Makes 4 servings

Estimated preparation time: 5 minutes
Chilling/cooling time: 2 hours
Cooking time: 10 minutes

Per serving: 762 calories, 79g protein, 40g fat (46% of calories), 26g carbohydrate, 202mg cholesterol, 628mg sodium, 8g dietary fiber

Fillet of Beef Andrea

Calzone Bake

A calzone full of the tastes of Italy—it's baked in a square for easy serving.

1 pound bulk pork sausage
1 can (15 ounces) PROGRESSO Tomato Sauce
1 can (14 ounces) PROGRESSO Artichoke Hearts, drained and
   chopped
2 cups (8 ounces) shredded mozzarella cheese, divided usage
½ teaspoon dried basil leaves
½ teaspoon dried oregano leaves
½ teaspoon garlic powder
2½ cups buttermilk baking mix
⅔ cup milk

1. Preheat oven to 350°F.

2. In large skillet, brown sausage; drain. Add tomato sauce, artichokes,
   1 cup cheese, basil, oregano and garlic powder; heat thoroughly, stirring
   occasionally. Remove from heat.

3. In small bowl, combine baking mix and milk; stir until mixture forms
   dough. Press half of dough onto bottom of 8-inch square baking dish.

4. Spoon sausage mixture over dough in baking dish.

5. Roll out remaining dough to 8-inch square; place on top of meat mixture.
   Sprinkle with remaining 1 cup cheese.

6. Bake 30 minutes.   Makes 6 servings

Estimated preparation time: 20 minutes
Baking time: 30 minutes

Per serving: 660 calories, 25g protein, 44g fat (60% of calories), 43g carbohydrate,
75mg cholesterol, 1959mg sodium, 4g dietary fiber

Meatballs with Creamy Mushroom Sauce

1 pound ground beef
½ cup PROGRESSO Italian Style Bread Crumbs
¼ cup chopped onion
1 egg, lightly beaten
1½ tablespoons PROGRESSO Olive Oil
1 can (18½ ounces) PROGRESSO Cream of Mushroom Soup
8 ounces egg noodles, cooked according to package directions

1. In medium bowl, combine ground beef, bread crumbs, onion and egg.

2. Shape meatballs using 1 level tablespoon meat mixture for each meatball.

3. In large skillet, heat olive oil. Add meatballs; cook 5 to 7 minutes or to desired doneness, turning occasionally to brown on all sides. Drain.

4. Pour soup over meatballs; cover. Simmer 10 minutes.

5. Serve meatballs over hot noodles. Makes 4 servings

Estimated preparation time: 15 minutes
Cooking time: 20 minutes

Per serving: 641 calories, 41g protein, 38g fat (53% of calories), 33g carbohydrate, 202mg cholesterol, 905mg sodium, 2g dietary fiber

Veal Cutlets Parmesan

¾ cup PROGRESSO Italian Style Bread Crumbs
6 tablespoons PROGRESSO Grated Parmesan Cheese, divided usage
¾ pound veal scaloppine, sliced ⅜ inch thick and pounded to ¼-inch thickness
2 eggs, lightly beaten
6 tablespoons PROGRESSO Olive Oil, divided usage
1 can (8 ounces) PROGRESSO Tomato Sauce
8 ounces sliced mozzarella cheese

1. Preheat oven to 350°F.

2. In shallow dish, combine bread crumbs and ¼ cup Parmesan cheese.

3. Dip veal into eggs; coat with bread crumb mixture. Place veal on platter; freeze 5 minutes or refrigerate 30 minutes.

4. In large skillet, heat 3 tablespoons olive oil over medium heat. Add half of the veal. Brown 2 minutes on each side; remove from skillet. Repeat with remaining olive oil and veal.

5. Place veal in 13×9-inch baking dish. Pour tomato sauce over veal; top with mozzarella cheese and remaining 2 tablespoons Parmesan cheese.

6. Bake 15 minutes or until hot and bubbly.

7. Broil 1 to 2 minutes to brown. Makes 4 servings

Estimated preparation time: 20 minutes
Chilling time: 30 minutes
Baking time: 16 minutes

Per serving: 758 calories, 47g protein, 55g fat (64% of calories), 24g carbohydrate, 257mg cholesterol, 1155mg sodium, 2g dietary fiber

Note: ¾ pound boneless, skinless chicken breast halves, pounded to ¼-inch thickness, may be substituted for veal.

Sausage and Lentil Stuffed Peppers

6 medium green or red bell peppers
1 pound bulk Italian sausage
½ cup chopped onion
1 can (10½ ounces) PROGRESSO Lentil Soup
1 cup cooked rice
¾ cup PROGRESSO Italian Style Bread Crumbs, divided usage
2 tablespoons PROGRESSO Grated Parmesan Cheese, divided usage
2 tablespoons butter, melted

1. Preheat oven to 350°F.

2. Fill large saucepan half-full with water; bring to a boil. Cut off tops of peppers; remove seeds. Place peppers in water. Boil 3 minutes; drain.

3. In large skillet, brown sausage and onion; drain. Stir in soup, rice, ½ cup bread crumbs and 1 tablespoon Parmesan cheese.

4. Fill peppers with sausage mixture; place in large shallow baking dish. Cover with foil.

5. Bake 25 minutes or until thoroughly heated. Remove foil.

6. In small bowl, combine butter, remaining ¼ cup bread crumbs and remaining 1 tablespoon Parmesan cheese. Sprinkle over peppers. Bake 5 minutes.   Makes 6 servings

Estimated preparation time: 20 minutes
Baking time: 30 minutes

Per serving: 440 calories, 21g protein, 26g fat (52% of calories), 32g carbohydrate, 71mg cholesterol, 1126mg sodium, 3g dietary fiber

Microwave Directions: Cut off tops of peppers; remove seeds. In 13×9-inch microwave-safe baking dish, place peppers and ¼ cup water; cover with plastic wrap, cutting a few slits in center of wrap to vent. Microwave on HIGH (100% power) 5 minutes, rotating dish after 3 minutes; drain. Crumble sausage into medium microwave-safe bowl; cover. Microwave on HIGH 5 minutes, stirring and breaking sausage into small pieces after 2½ minutes. Stir in onion. Microwave on HIGH 2 minutes; drain. Break up any remaining large pieces of sausage. Stir in soup, rice, ½ cup bread crumbs and 1 tablespoon Parmesan cheese. Fill peppers with sausage mixture. Return peppers to baking dish; cover. Microwave on MEDIUM (50% power) 15 minutes, rotating dish every 5 minutes. In small bowl, combine butter, remaining ¼ cup bread crumbs and remaining 1 tablespoon Parmesan cheese. Sprinkle over peppers. Microwave on HIGH 1 minute.

Sausage and Lentil Stuffed Peppers

Italian Marinated Steak

A well-seasoned marinade adds a nice flavor to steak, and later becomes a sauce.

1 can (19 ounces) PROGRESSO Tomato Soup, drained, reserving broth and soup pieces separately
2 tablespoons Burgundy wine
1 tablespoon Worcestershire sauce
¾ teaspoon Italian seasoning
½ teaspoon dry mustard
1¼ pounds boneless sirloin steak

1. In shallow 2-quart baking dish, combine reserved soup broth, wine, Worcestershire sauce, Italian seasoning and dry mustard; mix well.

2. Add steak to marinade; cover. Refrigerate 2 hours, turning steak occasionally. Remove steak from marinade, reserving marinade.

3. Bake, broil or grill steak to desired doneness, brushing frequently with reserved marinade.

4. In small saucepan, combine remaining marinade and soup pieces; bring to a boil. Serve over steak.   Makes 4 servings

Estimated preparation time: 10 minutes
Chilling/cooling time: 2 hours
Baking time: 10 minutes

Per serving: 355 calories, 45g protein, 13g fat (31% of calories), 11g carbohydrate, 126mg cholesterol, 680mg sodium, ‹1g dietary fiber

Breaded Veal Piccata

An example of the simplicity of Italian food. Italian cooks frequently use lemon to add a piquant flavor to a variety of dishes.

1 pound veal scaloppine, sliced ⅜ inch thick and pounded to ¼-inch thickness
2 eggs, lightly beaten
1¼ cups PROGRESSO Italian Style Bread Crumbs
6 tablespoons PROGRESSO Olive Oil, divided usage
2 tablespoons butter
1½ tablespoons all-purpose flour
¼ teaspoon salt
¼ teaspoon ground black pepper
¾ cup chicken broth
⅔ cup dry white wine
1 tablespoon freshly squeezed lemon juice

1. Dip veal into eggs; coat with bread crumbs. Place veal on platter; freeze 5 minutes or refrigerate 30 minutes.

2. In large skillet, heat 3 tablespoons olive oil over medium heat. Add half of the veal; brown 2 minutes on each side. Remove from skillet; keep warm. Repeat with remaining olive oil and veal.

3. Remove drippings and any remaining oil from skillet. Melt butter in skillet. Stir in flour, salt and pepper; cook 1 minute. Gradually add chicken broth, wine and lemon juice, stirring constantly until mixture comes to a boil and thickens slightly; boil 1 minute.

4. Return veal to skillet; simmer 2 to 3 minutes or until thoroughly heated.

Makes 4 servings

Estimated preparation time: 25 minutes
Chilling time: 30 minutes
Cooking time: 15 minutes

Per serving: 784 calories, 44g protein, 51g fat (61% of calories), 31g carbohydrate, 255mg cholesterol, 1004mg sodium, 1g dietary fiber

Note: 1 pound boneless, skinless chicken breast halves, pounded to ¼-inch thickness, may be substituted for veal.

Pork Cutlets Genovese

Spicy mustard adds a burst of flavor to these easy-to-prepare breaded cutlets.

¼ cup sour cream
2 tablespoons Dijon-style mustard
1 pound pork cutlets
⅔ cup PROGRESSO Italian Style Bread Crumbs
3 tablespoons PROGRESSO Olive Oil

1. In small bowl, combine sour cream and mustard.

2. Dip pork into sour cream mixture; coat with bread crumbs.

3. In large skillet, heat olive oil. Add pork; cook 10 to 15 minutes or until browned on both sides and pork is no longer pink in center.

Makes 4 servings

Estimated preparation time: 10 minutes
Cooking time: 15 minutes

Per serving: 467 calories, 40g protein, 27g fat (52% of calories), 16g carbohydrate, 118mg cholesterol, 514mg sodium, 1g dietary fiber

Stuffed Zucchini Italiano

4 medium zucchini (about 2 pounds)
1 pound ground beef
1 jar (30 ounces) PROGRESSO Marinara Spaghetti Sauce, divided usage
½ cup PROGRESSO Italian Style Bread Crumbs
⅓ cup PROGRESSO Grated Parmesan Cheese
1 teaspoon dried oregano leaves
½ teaspoon salt
⅛ teaspoon ground black pepper
1 egg, lightly beaten
⅓ cup shredded mozzarella cheese

1. Preheat oven to 375°F.

2. Trim ends of zucchini; cut in half lengthwise. Carefully scoop out centers, leaving ¼-inch thick shells. Chop pulp (makes about 1 cup); set aside.

3. In large skillet, brown ground beef; drain.

4. Add zucchini pulp, ½ cup marinara sauce, bread crumbs, Parmesan cheese, oregano, salt, pepper and egg to ground beef; mix well.

5. Place zucchini shells in shallow baking pan. Spoon ground beef mixture into shells.

6. Pour remaining marinara sauce over zucchini; cover.

7. Bake 30 to 35 minutes or until zucchini shells are tender. Remove cover.

8. Top with mozzarella cheese. Bake 5 minutes or until cheese is melted.

Makes 8 servings

Estimated preparation time: 30 minutes
Baking time: 40 minutes

Per serving: 338 calories, 25g protein, 20g fat (51% of calories), 17g carbohydrate, 94mg cholesterol, 831mg sodium, 1g dietary fiber

Microwave Directions: Prepare zucchini as directed above in Step 2. Crumble ground beef into medium microwave-safe container; cover. Microwave on HIGH (100% power) 4 minutes, stirring and breaking ground beef into small pieces after 2 minutes; drain. Break up any remaining large pieces of ground beef. Continue as directed above in Steps 4 through 6, *except* using a microwave-safe baking dish; cover with plastic wrap, cutting a few slits in center of wrap to vent. Microwave on HIGH 11 to 13 minutes or until zucchini shells are tender, rotating dish every 5 minutes. Remove plastic wrap. Top with mozzarella cheese; cover. Microwave on HIGH 1 to 2 minutes or until cheese is melted. Let stand 5 minutes before serving.

Stuffed Zucchini Italiano

Vegetable Pepperoni Pizza

The light tang of marinated vegetables gives special flair to this colorful pizza.

2 (12-inch) refrigerated pizza crusts
1 can (8 ounces) PROGRESSO Tomato Sauce
1 can (6 ounces) PROGRESSO Tomato Paste
½ teaspoon dried oregano leaves
½ teaspoon dried basil leaves
4 ounces pepperoni slices
1 jar (7 ounces) PROGRESSO Roasted Peppers (red), drained and sliced
1 jar (6 ounces) PROGRESSO Marinated Artichoke Hearts, drained and coarsely chopped
1 jar (6 ounces) PROGRESSO Marinated Mushrooms, drained and halved
2 cups (8 ounces) shredded mozzarella cheese
2 green onions, sliced
2 tablespoons PROGRESSO Grated Parmesan Cheese

1. Preheat oven to 400°F.

2. Place crusts on two lightly greased 12-inch pizza pans. Bake 8 minutes.

3. In small bowl, combine tomato sauce, tomato paste, oregano and basil. Spread half of sauce mixture onto each pizza crust.

4. Arrange pepperoni, roasted peppers, artichoke hearts and mushrooms over sauce mixture.

5. Top pizzas with mozzarella cheese, green onions and Parmesan cheese.

6. Bake 10 to 15 minutes or until cheese is melted and crusts are golden brown.

Makes 8 servings

Estimated preparation time: 15 minutes
Baking time: 15 minutes

Per serving: 441 calories, 17g protein, 22g fat (45% of calories), 43g carbohydrate, 29mg cholesterol, 940mg sodium, 4g dietary fiber

Variation:
Substitute pizza crust mix for refrigerated pizza crusts. Prepare enough dough to make two pizza crusts according to package directions; press dough onto bottoms of two greased pizza pans. Bake at 400°F, 8 minutes.

Cheese-Stuffed Meatloaf

A surprise center adds zest and color to this familiar favorite.

1½ pounds ground beef
¾ cup PROGRESSO Italian Style Bread Crumbs
½ teaspoon salt
¼ teaspoon ground black pepper
1 can (8 ounces) PROGRESSO Tomato Sauce
2 eggs, divided usage
¾ cup ricotta cheese
¼ cup PROGRESSO Grated Parmesan Cheese
¼ cup chopped fresh parsley

1. Preheat oven to 350°F.

2. In large bowl, combine ground beef, bread crumbs, salt, pepper, tomato sauce and one egg.

3. In small bowl, combine remaining egg, ricotta cheese, Parmesan cheese and parsley.

4. Press one third of the ground beef mixture into 9×4-inch loaf pan. Make shallow well lengthwise in center; spoon cheese mixture into well. Cover with remaining ground beef mixture; pat firmly at sides to seal.

5. Bake 1 hour. Let stand 5 minutes before slicing to serve.

Makes 6 servings

Estimated preparation time: 15 minutes
Baking time: 1 hour

Per serving: 525 calories, 42g protein, 32g fat (56% of calories), 16g carbohydrate, 211mg cholesterol, 843mg sodium, 1g dietary fiber

Microwave Directions: Prepare meatloaf as directed above in Steps 2 through 4, *except* using 9×4-inch microwave-safe loaf pan. Microwave on HIGH (100% power) 15 to 17 minutes or until internal temperature in center of meatloaf reaches 145°F, rotating dish after 8 minutes. Let stand 5 minutes before slicing to serve.

Seafood Dishes

Mediterranean-Style Crab Cakes

  5 tablespoons butter, divided usage
¼ cup chopped onion
¼ cup chopped celery
  1 clove garlic, minced
  2 cans (6 ounces each) crabmeat, well drained
1¼ cups PROGRESSO Italian Style Bread Crumbs, divided usage
¼ cup mayonnaise
  1 egg, lightly beaten
1½ teaspoons Worcestershire sauce
  1 teaspoon freshly squeezed lemon juice
⅛ teaspoon ground black pepper

1. In large skillet, heat 1 tablespoon butter. Add onion, celery and garlic; cook 3 minutes or until tender, stirring occasionally.

2. Remove skillet from heat. Stir in crabmeat, ¾ cup bread crumbs, mayonnaise, egg, Worcestershire sauce, lemon juice and pepper.

3. Shape crabmeat mixture into 4 patties; coat with remaining ½ cup bread crumbs, pressing crumbs onto each patty.

4. In same large skillet over medium heat, melt remaining 4 tablespoons butter. Cook patties in butter 8 to 9 minutes or until golden brown on both sides.   Makes 4 servings

Estimated preparation time: 15 minutes
Cooking time: 8 minutes

Per serving: 485 calories, 24g protein, 30g fat (56% of calories), 30g carbohydrate, 175mg cholesterol, 1004mg sodium, 1g dietary fiber

Mediterranean-Style Crab Cakes

Shrimp fra Diavolo

(Shrimp with Spicy Stuffing)

Everyone's favorite...shrimp. These are stuffed with a zesty crumb mixture and topped with marinara sauce.

1¾ pounds (about 24) shelled and deveined uncooked jumbo shrimp, with tails left on
¼ cup butter
1 jar (9 ounces) PROGRESSO Tuscan Peppers (pepperoncini), finely chopped and drained
1 cup finely chopped green onions
1 teaspoon PROGRESSO Garlic Puree
1 cup PROGRESSO Italian Style Bread Crumbs
½ cup crabmeat
2 hard cooked eggs, chopped
2 tablespoons PROGRESSO Grated Parmesan Cheese, divided usage
3 tablespoons PROGRESSO Olive Oil
1 jar (14 ounces) PROGRESSO Marinara Sauce

1. Preheat oven to 500°F.

2. Butterfly shrimp by slicing down length of underside, almost to vein.

3. In medium saucepan, melt butter. Add Tuscan peppers, green onions and garlic; cook 3 minutes, stirring occasionally. Remove from heat. Stir in bread crumbs, crabmeat, eggs and 1 tablespoon Parmesan cheese.

4. Spread 1½ cups stuffing over bottom of 13×9-inch baking dish.

5. Lay shrimp on flat surface with split side up. Spoon remaining stuffing into crevice of each shrimp, pressing stuffing into crevice.

6. Place shrimp, stuffing side up, in single layer over stuffing in dish; brush tops of shrimp with olive oil.

7. Bake 6 to 8 minutes or until shrimp turn pink.

8. In small pan, heat marinara sauce; drizzle over top of shrimp.

9. Sprinkle with remaining 1 tablespoon Parmesan cheese.

Makes 6 servings

Estimated preparation time: 1 hour
Cooking time: 8 minutes

Per serving: 455 calories, 37g protein, 23g fat (46% of calories), 26g carbohydrate, 304mg cholesterol, 885mg sodium, 1g dietary fiber

Shrimp fra Diavolo

Lobster Mushroom Sauce di Riso

1 can (10½ ounces) PROGRESSO Rock Lobster Spaghetti Sauce
¼ pound lobster meat (real or imitation), sliced ¼ inch thick (about
    ¾ cup)
⅓ cup sliced fresh mushrooms
2 teaspoons sherry
¾ teaspoon seafood seasoning
2 cups rice, cooked according to package directions
2 tablespoons PROGRESSO Grated Parmesan Cheese

1. In medium saucepan over medium heat combine rock lobster sauce, lobster, mushrooms, sherry and seafood seasoning; cook 5 to 8 minutes or until thoroughly heated, stirring occasionally.

2. Serve over rice. Sprinkle with cheese.   Makes 4 servings

Estimated preparation time: 10 minutes
Cooking time: 5 minutes

Per serving: 251 calories, 12g protein, 6g fat (23% of calories), 37g carbohydrate, 29mg cholesterol, 649mg sodium, 2g dietary fiber

Hot 'n Spicy Fish

2 tablespoons PROGRESSO Olive Oil
½ teaspoon hot pepper sauce
½ cup PROGRESSO Italian Style Bread Crumbs
½ teaspoon dried thyme leaves
½ teaspoon dried oregano leaves
¼ teaspoon cayenne pepper
1 pound fish fillets

1. In small bowl, combine olive oil and hot pepper sauce; set aside.

2. In shallow dish, combine bread crumbs and seasonings.

3. Lightly brush both sides of fish with olive oil mixture; coat with bread crumb mixture. Place on greased rack of broiler pan.

4. Broil, 4 to 5 inches from heat source, 5 minutes per side or until fish flakes easily with fork.   Makes 4 servings

Estimated preparation time: 10 minutes
Baking time: 10 minutes

Per serving: 224 calories, 23g protein, 9g fat (38% of calories), 11g carbohydrate, 54mg cholesterol, 332mg sodium, 1g dietary fiber

Lobster Mushroom Sauce di Riso

Broiled Shellfish Venetian-Style

An easy way to please seafood lovers...shrimp and scallops, crispy coated and broiled on skewers. Serve with a squeeze of lemon.

1 cup PROGRESSO Italian Style Bread Crumbs
⅓ cup PROGRESSO Olive Oil
1 pound peeled and deveined uncooked shrimp
1 pound sea scallops
   Lemon wedges

1. In small bowl, combine bread crumbs and olive oil.

2. In large bowl or large plastic bag, combine shrimp and scallops. Add bread crumb mixture; toss gently to coat shellfish. Cover. Refrigerate 1 hour.

3. Thread shellfish onto skewers. Place on greased rack of broiler pan.

4. Broil, 3 inches from heat source, 5 minutes or until crisp and golden brown on both sides, turning every 2 minutes. *Do not overcook.* Serve with lemon wedges.

Makes 6 servings

Estimated preparation time: 15 minutes
Chilling/cooling time: 1 hour
Cooking time: 5 minutes

Per serving: 332 calories, 31g protein, 16g fat (42% of calories), 17g carbohydrate, 140mg cholesterol, 554mg sodium, 1g dietary fiber

Variation:
Thread skewers with fresh mushrooms, cherry tomatoes, onion chunks and parboiled bell pepper chunks. Broil, 3 inches from heat source, 3 minutes or until vegetables are tender, turning every minute.

Broiled Shellfish Venetian-Style

Desserts

Layered Fruit Cheesecake

Prepared bread crumbs make a perfect crust for this creamy cheesecake, sparked with a layer of tart cranberry.

1 Bread Crumb Dessert Crust for filled crust (p. 92)
2 packages (8 ounces each) cream cheese, softened
2 eggs
¾ cup sugar
1 can (8 ounces) crushed pineapple, drained
1 can (16 ounces) whole berry cranberry sauce, divided usage

1. Preheat oven to 350°F.

2. In large bowl, beat together cream cheese, eggs and sugar on high speed of electric mixer until well blended.

3. Stir in pineapple; pour half of mixture into crust.

4. Spoon 1 cup cranberry sauce over cream cheese mixture in crust; top with remaining cream cheese mixture. Reserve and chill remaining cranberry sauce for garnish.

5. Bake 40 to 45 minutes or until edge is light golden brown; cool completely on wire rack. Refrigerate until chilled, at least 4 hours or overnight. Garnish with reserved cranberry sauce.

Makes 8 servings

Estimated preparation time: 20 minutes
Baking time: 45 minutes
Chilling/cooling time: 4 hours

Per serving: 549 calories, 8g protein, 30g fat (48% of calories), 66g carbohydrate, 136mg cholesterol, 313mg sodium, 2g dietary fiber

Layered Fruit Cheesecake

Cassata alla Bread Crumbs

(Almond Trifle)

This light-textured dessert is much easier to make than it looks.

1½ cups PROGRESSO Plain Bread Crumbs
 ½ cup all-purpose flour
 1 tablespoon baking powder
 ¼ teaspoon salt
 1 cup sugar
 ½ cup butter, softened
 3 eggs
 1 cup milk
 1 teaspoon vanilla extract
 5 tablespoons amaretto, divided usage
 ½ cup maraschino cherry halves
 ½ cup plus 1 tablespoon sliced almonds
 1 container (8 ounces) LA CREME Whipped Topping, thawed

1. Preheat oven to 350°F.

2. In small bowl, combine bread crumbs, flour, baking powder and salt.

3. In large bowl, beat together sugar and butter on medium speed of electric mixer until light and fluffy. Add eggs, one at a time, beating well after each addition. With mixer on low speed, alternately add bread crumb mixture and milk to sugar mixture. Blend in vanilla.

4. Pour batter evenly into two greased and floured 8-inch square baking dishes.

5. Bake 20 to 25 minutes or until cake tester inserted in centers comes out clean. Cool on wire racks.

6. Sprinkle 1 tablespoon amaretto over each cake; cut into ½-inch cubes.

7. Reserve a few cherries for garnish, if desired. In large glass serving bowl, spoon one fourth of the whipped topping. Top with layers of one third each of the cake cubes, remaining cherries and almonds; sprinkle with 1 tablespoon amaretto. Repeat layers of whipped topping, cake cubes, cherries, almonds and amaretto two more times. Top with remaining whipped topping. Garnish with reserved cherries.

8. Chill at least 2 hours before serving.   Makes 10 servings

Estimated preparation time: 30 minutes
Baking time: 25 minutes
Chilling/cooling time: 3 hours

Per serving: 463 calories, 7g protein, 21g fat (46% of calories), 55g carbohydrate, 96mg cholesterol, 334mg sodium, 2g dietary fiber

Cassata alla Bread Crumbs

Berry-Oat Squares

2 cups rolled oats
1½ cups PROGRESSO Plain Bread Crumbs
1 cup packed brown sugar
1 cup chopped nuts
1 can (16 ounces) whole berry cranberry sauce
½ cup PET Evaporated Milk
¼ cup butter, melted

1. Preheat oven to 350°F.

2. In large bowl, combine all ingredients; mix well. Spread into greased 13×9-inch baking dish.

3. Bake 35 to 40 minutes or until golden brown; cool. Cut into squares.

Makes 2 dozen

Estimated preparation time: 10 minutes
Baking time: 40 minutes

Per 1 square serving: 175 calories, 3g protein, 6g fat (32% of calories), 28g carbohydrate, 8mg cholesterol, 70mg sodium, 2g dietary fiber

Bread Crumb Dessert Crust

A toasty crumb crust far better than store-bought, and so easy to make.

1 cup PROGRESSO Plain Bread Crumbs
¼ cup packed brown sugar
⅓ cup butter or margarine, melted

For unfilled baked crust:
1. Preheat oven to 350°F.

2. In medium bowl, combine bread crumbs and brown sugar. Add butter; mix well with fork. Press crumb mixture into 9-inch pie plate.

3. Bake 8 to 9 minutes or until lightly browned; cool on wire rack. Fill as desired.

For filled crust:
1. Preheat oven and prepare filling as directed in your recipe.

2. Combine crust ingredients; press into 9-inch pie plate.

3. Pour filling into crust. Bake according to recipe directions.

Makes 1 (9-inch) pie crust

Estimated preparation time: 5 minutes
Baking time for empty crust: 8 minutes

Per ⅛ of pie crust serving: 153 calories, 2g protein, 9g fat (50% of calories), 18g carbohydrate, 20mg cholesterol, 113mg sodium, ‹1g dietary fiber

Index

METRIC CONVERSION CHART

VOLUME MEASUREMENT*

1/8 teaspoon = 0.5 mL
1/4 teaspoon = 1 mL
1/3 teaspoon = 1 mL
1/2 teaspoon = 2 mL
3/4 teaspoon = 4 mL
1 teaspoon = 5 mL
½ tablespoon = 7 mL
1 tablespoon = 15 mL
1½ tablespoons = 22 mL
2 tablespoons = 25 mL
3 tablespoons = 45 mL
1/4 cup = 50 mL
1/3 cup = 80 mL
1/2 cup = 125 mL
2/3 cup = 160 mL
3/4 cup = 180 mL
1 cup = 250 mL (236.58)
1½ cups = 375 mL
2 cups = 1 pt. = 500 mL
2½ cups = 625 mL
3 cups = 750 mL
3½ cups = 825 mL
4 cups = 1 qt. = 1 L
1 fluid ounce (2 Tbs.) = 30 mL
4 fluid ounces (½ cup) = 125 mL
8 fluid ounces (1 cup) = 250 mL
12 fluid ounces (1½ cups) = 375 mL
16 fluid ounces (2 cups) = 500 mL
*(including fluid ounces)

WEIGHT (MASS)*

½ ounce = 15 g
1 ounce = 30 g (28.35)
2 ounces = 60 g
3 ounces = 85 g
4 ounces = 115 g
8 ounces = 225 g

BAKING PAN SIZES

Utensil	Metric Volume	Metric Measure in cm	Closest Size in Inches or Volume
Baking or Cake Pan	2 L	20 x 5	8 x 2
	2.5 L	22 x 5	9 x 2
	3 L	30 x 20 x 5	12 x 8 x 2
	3.5 L	33 x 23 x 5	13 x 9 x 2
Loaf Pan	1.5 L	20 x 10 x 7	8 x 4 x 3
	2 L	23 x 13 x 7	9 x 5 x 3
Round Layer Cake Pan	1.2 L	20 x 4	8 x 1½
	1.5 L	23 x 4	9 x 1½
Pie Pan	750 mL	20 x 3	8 x 1¼
	1 L	23 x 3	9 x 1¼
Baking Dish or Casserole	1 L		1 qt.
	1.5 L		1½ qt.
	2 L		2 qt.

12 ounces = 340 g
16 ounces = 1 lb. = 450 g
2 pounds = 900 g
*Ounces to Grams

DIMENSION

1/16 inch = 2 mm
1/8 inch = 0.5 cm
3/16 inch = 0.5 cm
1/4 inch = 0.5 cm
3/8 inch = 1 cm
1/2 inch = 1.5 cm
5/8 inch = 1.5 cm
3/4 inch = 2 cm
1 inch = 2.5 cm (2.54)

1½ inches = 4 cm
2 inches = 5 cm

OVEN TEMPERATURES

250° F = 120° C
275° F = 140° C
300° F = 150° C
325° F = 160° C
350° F = 180° C
375° F = 190° C
400° F = 200° C
425° F = 220° C
450° F = 230° C
*(− 32 x 5 ÷ 9) (low temps. do exact conversion)